The Gospel of Now

The
Gospel
of Now

Vincent P. McCorry, S.J.

Herder and Herder

1968
HERDER AND HERDER NEW YORK
232 Madison Avenue, New York, N.Y. 10016

Nihil obstat: Brendan W. Lawlor, Censor Librorum
Imprimatur: ✠Robert F. Joyce, Bishop of Burlington
July 24, 1968

Grateful acknowledgement is made to The America Press for permission to reprint the materials contained in this book, all of which originally appeared in *America* magazine.

Library of Congress Catalog Card Number: 68–55087
© 1968 by Herder and Herder, Inc.
Manufactured in the United States

Contents

The Gospel of Now

Revelation and History

Brethren, already it is high time for us to awake out of our sleep; our salvation is closer to us now than when we first learned to believe. . . . When all this begins, look up, and lift up your heads; it means that the time draws near for your deliverance. (Romans 13:11 and Luke 21:28; Epistle and Gospel of the First Sunday of Advent)

On the first Sunday of a new ecclesiastical year, we notice liturgical mention, first by St. Paul, then by Christ Himself, of *time*. The references will introduce a matter that may serve us well for Advent reflection.

One of the problems involved in the bottomless mystery of God is that of communication. How does man communicate with the God whom he does not see or, in the ordinary sense, hear? How does the invisible, silent God speak to man?

Obviously, man can speak to God in prayer. At once there arises the question that so vexes religious man in his search for God. When man prays, is God really listening? When I talk to God, does it not seem—and often seem—that I am only talking to myself, or, at best, reciting a dead formula? If prayer is genuine communication, should not a man at prayer experience some sense of that Other with whom he is seeking contact?

On the testimony of history, there has also been in religious man (and man has been religious, one way or another, with impressive consistency) a conviction or intuition that he can communicate with God by way of gift-giving—that is, by the religious act of sacrifice. As in the case of prayer, man has been understandably eager to know whether God is pleased with man's present, and truly receives it.

Then there is the other side of the problem. How does God speak to us? In particular, is there such a thing as objective divine revelation? If so, what has been the mode of that revelation? Has God spoken to us through natural forces like flood and fire and storm and drought, and even in the language of the ever changing seasons? Or has God spoken to us in history? To communicate with man, has God actually intervened in time, in human event that takes place in time and therefore adds a new significance to time itself?

It is said by those who know such matters best that the Hebrew people were the first to see time as linear rather than cyclic, to conceive history not as a perpetual reiteration but as a succession of events with a beginning and an end, all in accordance with a divine plan. "If Israel has broken with the cyclic concept of time," writes Canadian priest-scholar René Latourelle, "the reason is that it has found God *in history*. Israel proclaims that God has intervened in its history, that this meeting took place on a certain day, and that this meeting has completely changed its existence. . . . History is, then, the place of revelation."

From such a view of the mode of divine revelation, certain highly significant conclusions follow. First, man becomes the master of time, for time is no longer a pointless, fatidic circle of seasons and meaningless happenings. Second, God's revelation becomes extremely factual; the transcendent divine is actualized, is made near and clear, grows solid and compelling.

Third: the conviction of history as revelation and revelation as history is the matrix of the whole concept of an Advent.

Event and Prophet

What was it, then, that you went out to see? A prophet? Yes, and something more, I tell you, than a prophet. (Matthew 11:9; Gospel of the Second Sunday of Advent)

It is both Hebrew and Christian conviction that almighty God reveals Himself to men, and in a particular way: in and through events. At successive moments and always with supreme freedom, God intervenes in history to make Himself and His truth known. Revelation itself has, therefore, a history; consequently, so has salvation. Revelation is first a matter of fact, then a matter of doctrine.

In the Jewish view, God had revealed Himself, had spoken to men—Israel was appointed to relay God's message to the whole world—in three huge events: the exodus, the covenant and the entrance into the promised land.

The central point of the Jewish escape from the geno-
cidal slavery of Egypt was not simply salvation, but salvation by the hand, the stretched-out arm, of Yahweh. It was
God who forced the capitulation of Pharaoh, God who
destroyed the pursuing Egyptian army, God who led Israel
by day and by night. As the exodus revealed God as
Saviour, the covenant in the desert established the sacred
and highly personal relationship between God and His
chosen people. Finally, the unlikely gift of the promised
land, a land flowing with milk and honey but strongly
defended against invasion, manifested Yahweh as completely faithful to His part in the covenant and stood as a
reminder that Israel must be faithful to its part, Israel
must obey Yahweh's code of obligations.

Thus, for Israel, did God reveal Himself in history.
Naturally, a question of considerable import arises. How
are men to know that God is speaking to them through
events? Granted that divine Providence rules all happenings while leaving men utterly free to structure those happenings, how are we to read God in history? How are we
to know what God is saying, revealing, to us in what
events?

Event as revelation stands incomplete without the
prophet. One of the achievements of the dynamic theology
of our day has been to provide new understanding of the
vital function of the prophet in the dealings of God with
men and of men with God. Even when they do not heed
him, men are deeply impressed by a prophet. While they
persecute him, they are unnerved by him. After they have
killed him, they are haunted by him. We all know so well
that we need someone to speak to us for God, in His name,

with His voice and authority. The evangelical narrative of the transfiguration of Christ remains mysterious, but at least we now look with respect upon the figures of Moses and Elias as they converse with the radiant Lord Christ.

Of course, a final element must be added to event and prophet if history is to become in fact revelation, if God's word to men is to bear fruit. That element is faith. The event takes place and is known. Sent by God, the prophet speaks, illuminating the known event: *Thus says the Lord . . . A message from the Lord . . .* It remains for men to believe.

Here is where revelation so often breaks down. But why do men refuse credence to God's word? Why do they ridicule the prophet as he lightens the event so manifestly heavy with mystery? Is it always because of natural and reasonable and healthy skepticism? Or is it rather because men obscurely fear that God's message will be a burden and a contradiction to them?

There, by Jordan banks, for all to see and hear, stood John, called the Baptist. *What was it, then, that you went out to see? A prophet? Yes . . .*

The Apex of Revelation

John answered them, I am baptizing you with water; but there is one standing in your midst of whom you know nothing; he it is who, though he comes after me, takes rank before me. (John 1:26–27; Gospel of the Third Sunday of Advent)

Revelation not only has a history; it has a history that mounts to an apex. God spoke to a chosen people in successive events: the exodus, the covenanting in the desert, the attainment of a promised land; and spokesmen for God—the prophets—proclaimed the message, in those happenings, of the Lord almighty.

As revelation proceeds, a certain notion, perception, conviction, grows steadily stronger and clearer. It is the idea that God has yet more to say to men and to do for them. There will be another and more perfect salvation, a new covenant will be struck between God and man, a more exalted Servant of Yahweh will appear, one who will be the bearer of God's final word. God's people never tired of rehearsing what God had spoken to them and what He had done for them in the past. But their eyes were fixed on the future, when God would speak to them and provide for them as never before.

Here is the solemn declaration with which the Epistle to the Hebrews opens: *In old days, God spoke to our fathers in many ways and by many means, through the prophets; now at last in these times he has spoken to us, with a Son to speak for him; a Son whom he has appointed to inherit all things, just as it was through him that he created this world of time; a Son who is the radiance of his Father's splendor, and the full expression of his being; all creation depends, for its support, on his enabling word.*

It was the Jewish claim that God's revelation to men would reach a climax. It is the Christian claim that revelation has done that: in Jesus, the Christ, the Son of God.

Two questions arise, of course. The first concerns the "particularism" of divine revelation. Why should a just and even-handed God make Himself particularly known to a particular nation? Isn't the notion of a chosen people inherently invidious? Why did God speak to Jews rather than to Eskimos or Bantus or the ancient, gifted people of China?

The most general and yet most final answer to the difficulty is that God is God; He knows quite well what He is doing, is supremely free to do it. More concretely, however, if God is going to make Himself known through history, then He will speak in His wisdom to and through a receptive culture that will itself be a powerful instrument of His communication. The history—even in its tragic aspect—and rich endowments of the Jewish people suggest that the particularism of God's revealing Himself is thoroughly justified. Thirdly, it must never be forgotten that whenever God makes a special choice among men, He chooses not for privilege but for service. That service will be rendered at heavy cost.

The other question is that of the authenticity of Jesus of Nazareth as a prophet of God, as *the* prophet of God, as the natural Son of God. Here, obviously, is the parting of the ways for Jew and Christian. Since a final answer to the question can be given only on the basis of religious faith, one grieves now that in the past men persecuted one another for such religious faith or the lack of it. Perhaps one of the sanest of religious realizations of the contemporary world is that no man should be punished for his faith or embarrassed by it.

The liturgical season of Advent strongly reminds the Christian of his definitive position, both in inward faith and outward profession, with regard to that opening declaration of the Epistle to the Hebrews.

The First and Last Word

Prepare the way of the Lord, straighten out his paths. Every valley is to be bridged, and every mountain and hill leveled, and the windings are to be cut straight, and the rough paths made into smooth roads; and all mankind is to see the saving power of God. (Luke 3:5–6; quoted from Isaiah 40:3–4; Gospel of the Fourth Sunday of Advent)

Divine revelation, the speaking of God to man, reaches its crest, its climax and its conclusion in God's Son become man. God's final and most perfect word to us is, fittingly, God's Word. Hear once more the sonorous, triumphant exordium of the Epistle to the Hebrews: *In old days, God spoke to our fathers in many ways and by many means, through the prophets; now at last in these times he has spoken to us, with a Son to speak for him; a Son, whom he has appointed to inherit all things, just as it was through him that he created this world of time; a Son, who is the radiance of his Father's splendor, and the full expression of his being.*

What has God's Son revealed to us? He has revealed God; and God's truth; and God's will.

There is an element in the revelation made by Christ that is utterly unique. Christ is both God revealing and God revealed. Who can tell us, with as much precision and exactness as we can bear, what God is really like? Obviously, only God. It is the evangelist John who most boldly trumpets this gigantic truth: *No man has ever gone up into heaven; but there is one who has come down from heaven, the Son of Man, who dwells in heaven.* And again: *The Son cannot do anything of his own impulse, he can only do what he sees his Father doing; what the Father does is what the Son does in his turn. The Father loves the Son, and discloses to him all that he himself does. . . . As the Father has within him the gift of life, so he has granted to the Son that he too should have within him the gift of life.*

This unparalleled feature of our Lord's revelation dictates the very terms in which He conveys His message. The point has been made again and again. When the prophets delivered the tidings with which they were charged, their signature was always the same, for it was not *their* signature; it was *Thus says the Lord almighty.* Nowhere do we find these words on the lips of Christ. Simply and quietly He declares: *I say to you.*

This one Man, precisely because He is so much more than man, can tell us with authority—a quality that was noticed in His teaching—the religious truths that God proposes for our belief. The uniqueness of the situation reappears, for our Lord not only teaches truth, He can say and did say: *I am truth.* "In this respect," writes Scripture scholar René Latourelle, "Christ cannot possibly be compared with Buddha, Confucius, Mohammed or any other founder of a religion. In the other religions, the doctrine and the object of the doctrine are distinguished from the founder. Here, on the contrary, the doctrine of Christ has Christ for its object. Our faith is faith in Christ as God; salvation is an option for or against Christ."

The case is the same for our Saviour's imperatives. When He bids us pray, and forgive injuries, and love that neighbor, and stop worrying, and be clean even in thought and desire, and not love money, and all the rest, He is telling us exactly what God desires and demands of us. Anyone who wishes may, for any number of reasons, keep a safe distance between himself and the moral directives of Christ. Only let him not enter a claim that he means life to be governed by the will of God.

What is God like? Look at Christ. What truths are God's truths? Listen to Christ. What does God want us to do? Find out from Christ. Can we be sure of God's love? Says Fr. Schillebeeckx: Christ is the "coming of God's love into visibility."

A Saviour Is Born

But the angel said to them: Do not be afraid; behold I bring you good news of a great rejoicing for the whole people. This day, in the city of David, a Saviour has been

born to you, the Lord Christ himself. (Luke 2:10–11;
Gospel of the First Nativity Mass)

Let Christmas be a festival of confidence.

A man may be confident for any number of reasons:
because he has money or influence, because he is widely
traveled or knows how to cope with the most arrogant
headwaiter, because he knows or thinks he knows more
than others about some subject, even because of physical
well-being or moral narrowness—perhaps even because he
has never outgrown the absurd vanity of youth. The confidence that flows from the Christ-Mass has nothing to do
with any of this. It is more nearly the antithesis of all
natural and therefore ill-founded self-confidence.

*This day, in the city of David, a Saviour has been born
to you.* The festival of the Nativity of *the Lord Christ
himself* is a fresh reminder that almighty God considers
us worth saving.

For all its evident shallowness, self-complacency in man
is next to incorrigible. There is not one of us who is not
secretly persuaded that, after all, when all is said and done,
in the final analysis, when the last bit of evidence is in,
there is really something sound and rather fine about
the heart and core of him. Nevertheless: when a man in
middle years finds himself glancing back over the general
and particular conduct of a life now more than half spent,
his instinctive and precious vanity may take a hard knock.
Indeed (to alter the figure slightly), it may be swamped
by a dark, bitter tide of self-abhorrence. Face to face with
his unimpressive accomplishments and his generally spotty
record, the grown and now occasionally faltering man will

stand in a certain danger—danger it is—of questioning
the whole worth and significance of his one existence on
the face of this green and sunlit earth.

Then comes Christmas. *This day, in the city of David,
a Saviour has been born to you.*

This day? Yes; for what happened all those long years
ago *in the city of David*—"O little town of Bethlehem!"—
happened with such decisive permanence, with such final
meaning, that it goes on happening at every Christmas
and in truth at every moment.

A Saviour? Ah, there is the point, there is the radiant,
transfiguring truth, there is the *good news of a great
rejoicing for the whole people!* One has been sent to us
not by any mundane authority, not from the most philan-
thropic human source, but by and from the omnipotent
and most merciful and most loving God—not to soothe or
hearten or even toughen us momentarily in our mortal
groping, but to *save* us: to justify and redeem and crown
our brief earthly existence with an eternity of unflawed
happiness.

Who is this *Saviour?* It is none other than *the Lord
Christ himself,* the only-begotten Son of God. I turn from
the sight of my wretched self not only with smarting,
stinging disappointment, but with angry revulsion. What
price, I secretly ask with contempt, shall be put upon
this single, silly individual who is no better and perhaps
little worse than millions of other sons and daughters of
bumbling Adam?

Almighty God answers me in the wordless wail of the
new-born Saviour. "The price I put upon you is—My
only-begotten Son."

Glad Beyond Measure

And all at once the star that [the Magi] had seen in the East was there going before them, till at last it stood still over the place where the child was. They, when they saw the star, were glad beyond measure. (Matthew 2:9–10; Gospel of the Epiphany)

The liturgical calendar of the present year observes four Sundays in the Epiphany season. We would like to devote this time to some consideration of what is termed the *infancy narrative* in the Gospel witness to Christ, the world's Saviour.

As we read again St. Matthew's story of the Magi, we feel once more the familiar warmth that flows from that inimitable narrative. How very wise were those Wise Men, how courageous, how splendidly tenacious! We fret again as those swarthy faces and burning eyes scan the night sky for the elusive, enigmatic star; once more with those dedicated searchers we are *glad beyond measure* when at last the bright star returns to guide them to their journey's priceless end.

And then we sigh. The star has disappeared, indeed. The Magi who bested Herod the Great have been done in by footnotes and *Wissenschaft*. The scientists of Scripture have deprived us of the only scientists mentioned in the four Gospels.

Here is the reason for some present reflection on the Gospel account of the infancy of our beloved Saviour. Is it really true that the best we can say of the Wise Men now is: "We mourn our loss," and that the least we feel inclined to say to the Scripture people is: "Go home, *periti*"?

All the good folk who long to cultivate the Christ of the Gospels, the Christ of the earliest Christian witness, the Christ described in words by the very Spirit of God, will do well to consider carefully and with open mind a single distinction that is made by responsible biblical scholarship.

Two kinds of narrative are found in the pages of Scripture. *Historical narrative* intends to communicate to us a series of connected events exactly or more approximately as they took place. This strict chronicle answers the question "What happened?" But there is also such a thing as *theological narrative*. This is a story that, though it bears the look and sound of a straightforward recitation of history, is not actually so. The inspired writer is communicating not a precise event, but a theological truth in the form of a narrative.

One thinks immediately of the story form that our Lord Himself so freely used in His teaching: the parable. But the special point now is that a Scripture narrative, even when it is not labeled as parable, may be largely that. If, after such a "history," we were to ask the Evangelist: "Now, is this what *really* happened?" the inspired one (who never dreamed of himself as a reporter in the modern sense) would only look away uncomfortably and shuffle his feet—the blessed feet of him who proclaims peace—and murmur: "But don't you see what I *mean?*"

Let the eminent Fr. Karl Rahner have the last word here: "So this day is the feast of the blessed journey of the man who seeks God on his life's pilgrimage, the journey of the man who finds God because he seeks Him."

The Quiet, Kind Companion

Seeing him there, they were full of wonder, and his mother said to him, My Son, why have you treated us so? Think, what anguish of mind your father and I have endured, searching for you. (Luke 2:48; Gospel of the Feast of the Holy Family)

Even as, on this most apt and appealing liturgical festival, we offer congratulations and admiration (both boundless) to good families everywhere, we wish to pay special attention to the plain man who was the head of the Holy Family.

About the early history of Joseph of Nazareth we possess a single fact. He was *of David's clan and family.* It is not likely that Joseph was overly impressed with his royal ancestry, but, being true Jew, his would not have been unaware of his Davidic blood. The consciousness may have nerved him to seek marriage with that splendid girl, Mary. At any rate, we are in possession of other facts about Joseph, and they merit consideration.

Joseph of Nazareth was acquainted with responsibility, well acquainted with trouble. When we speak of Joseph as head of the Holy Family, we are not bestowing or repeating an honorary title. The Gospel of Matthew makes it painfully clear that divine directives for the Holy Family were delivered to Joseph, not to Mary. What is more, the heavenly instructions not only presumed and demanded energetic action on the part of Joseph, but they left more than enough room for personal decisions. Fathers of families—and mothers, too—should be steadied by the sure knowledge that St. Joseph met the heaviest kind of responsibility with courage and decisiveness.

As for troubles, poor Joseph must have developed a kind of expertise in the matter. His trial with regard to our Lady's chastity was singularly cruel; he probably felt that he had somehow bungled arrangements at Bethlehem; he lived through the terror of the flight from vicious Herod; he had to make a family living in a strange land; he led the way back to Israel in fear of one of Herod's fierce sons; he must surely have felt responsible for the loss of the 12-year-old Jesus. Trouble? Name it, and Joseph had it.

Now this heavy fact has particular bearing on something else we know about Joseph, and the juxtaposition or relationship constitutes something of a marvel. The Gospels record not a single word uttered by Joseph. The Evangelists, as we understand, made use of already existing materials when, under divine inspiration, they wrote the Gospels. Was there no record anywhere of anything said by Joseph? When he learned the sublime truth about Mary's pregnancy, when our Lord was born, on the terrible night of the escape, when the Boy was found in the temple—on all these momentous occasions did Joseph say nothing?

We can only conclude that he said little while he did much. Apparently he was not one for loud complaining, and he had ample grounds for complaint. Evidently he was the kind of man who does not particularly raise his voice, does not flagellate people with his opinions, does not make a career of talking—especially about himself. And here is the reason why, if the Christian second half of the 20th century needs a patron saint, the choice should fall upon Joseph of Nazareth. Amid the fearful cacophony of transistor radio, portable television, urban racket and booming beliefs (nonreligious, of course), no one seems able either to find or keep quiet anymore.

Good Joseph, family man, complete man, brave man, quiet man, gentle man: please pray for us.

Crisis at a Wedding

*Jesus himself, and his disciples, had also been invited to
the wedding. Here the supply of wine failed; whereupon
Jesus' mother said to him: They have no wine left. Jesus
answered her . . .* (John 2:3–4; Gospel for the Second
Sunday after Epiphany)

It wasn't a big wedding. Naturally, there was the usual
week of festivities, but these people were country folk,
not at all sophisticated or affluent, and they had calculated
the whole business somewhat closely. Then, in the middle
of it all, the newcomers from Judea had walked in. They
were six in number—most of them brave trenchermen,
who never refused another small measure of wine either.

It wasn't as if they weren't welcome—especially Mary's
Son, now a tall, grown man. But no one had been sure
that He, much less His new and rather plain friends,
would appear. Appear they did, and before long you
could feel worry circulating like a current of cold air.
There are certain deficiencies that simply must not occur
at a wedding feast, and the worst one of all was beginning
to be suspected at this wedding feast.

The whole male company was sitting more or less
merrily at dinner on the day following the arrival of the
late guests, but the talk was not what it had been. The

groom scarcely looked the part. He was trying to eat, and pretending not to notice the empty cups on the tables. On either side of him, his father and his bride's father struggled to converse with their nearest neighbor.

At the foot of one of the tables, the biggest of the arrivals from the south, the one they called Simon, was telling how sumptuously weddings were celebrated—he recalled his own—in his home town, Capharnaum. At another table Mary's Son was sitting quietly. He appeared to have a drop of wine left in His cup, for occasionally He raised it to His lips.

And then it happened very quickly. Mary of Nazareth came out of the kitchen—a graceful and quiet woman—carrying a tray as if to gather up dishes. But she made straight for where her Son was sitting, and standing behind Him, leaning a little toward Him, she said something in a low voice. He turned immediately, and for a moment His face lit up as it always did when He saw His Mother.

Then His expression went blank, even a mite severe. He talked briefly, earnestly, to His Mother. She said nothing, just stood there looking at Him. For a minute it was like a tableau: the two of them seemed unaware that everyone was watching them.

And then the Son of Mary smiled. He made a slight movement as if shrugging His shoulders. His Mother smiled back—and at her smile the whole room grew bright. She put out her hand and laid it for a moment on her Son's shoulder. Then she turned back to the kitchen only pausing to say a word to the waiters who were standing uncertainly together. Her Son was already rising from His place.

In short order the feast was a real feast again. Every wine cup was filled and filled again. The man named Simon was saying that Cana wasn't such a bad place, after all. And the lynx-eyed man on the left of Mary's Son, clutching his cup, was vehemently telling Him how much he would have made on this year's crops if his rock-headed brother hadn't bungled the whole deal.

In a moment of quiet someone said what everyone was thinking: "There you are. She can do anything with Him."

Religion: A Mystery

When he heard that, Jesus said to his followers in amazement: Believe me, I have not found faith like this, even in Israel. (Matthew 8:10; Gospel for the Third Sunday after Epiphany)

Amazing, indeed, is the amazement of the Lord Christ. One turns to a ponderous lexicon and reads that *amazement* means "mental stupefaction, bewilderment, consternation, overwhelming wonder." The bemused commentator then seeks out, in an even more ponderous volume, the occurrence of the word in Scripture. He thus discovers eleven cases of amazement in the Old Testament—not surprising, really—and five in the New. Twice the multitudes are *amazed* at our Lord's miracles; in Acts the crowds are *amazed* both on the first Pentecost morning and when Peter and John cure the crippled man; and the companions of fire-breathing Saul of Tarsus are *amazed* when their hero is abruptly flattened outside Damascus.

This is all very well; it makes perfectly good sense. But how are we to equate the interior reactions of the Incarnate Word with those of gaping throngs of highly impressionable people when they witness some prodigy they never dreamed of and cannot comprehend?

No doubt one should not raise questions he cannot honestly answer. Even when conducted in all reverence, probing into the psychology of the God-Man is an uncommonly thankless business. All such diagnostic investigation must proceed on the principle of parity: I feel wretched when I look a fool: so, most probably, do you. But there is simply not the remotest kind of parallel to God-made-man. So, then, three brief remarks must suffice in our present question: (1) Christ our Lord was truly and perfectly man; He is most certainly one of us, and up to a point reacts as we normally would. (2) Expert contemporary studies of the Saviour, without pretending to solve the insoluble and, of course, without at all questioning the divine element, tend distinctly to stress the human in Christ. (3) If the Gospel says that our Lord spoke *in amazement,* He did.

What is more rewarding in this matter is to inquire not how but why our most serene Lord was thus astonished.

The centurion (master-sergeant? warrant-officer?) of this miracle was not a Roman, neither was he a Jew. He may have been a Syrian or an Arab, and he was in the pay of the prince of Galilee, *that fox,* Herod Antipas. On the face of it, this soldier was not a man in whom one would look for deep supernatural faith. Moreover, as has often been observed, this religious faith was enforced and implemented by most authentic charity; for the sick person for whom the centurion pleads is a *servant,* that is, a slave.

It is of this professional soldier that the Son of God speaks *in amazement.* It is of this pagan, no son of *Abraham and Isaac and Jacob,* that the Saviour of the world says: *Believe me, I have not found faith like this, even in Israel.*

The moral of this Gospel incident is writ clear, and must be fairly and not infrequently weighed by sincere religious folk. Religion is not magic. Religion does not immediately solve all problems, answer all questions, confer all virtues. It can be disconcerting to observe what is observable: that life-long, energetic practice of religion will leave some people habitual liars, cowards, gluttons, malingerers, misers, slanderers. It is disturbing to acknowledge that religion is apt to suffer most, in the image it suggests, from some of its most conspicuous adherents.

It will not altogether serve to draw a distinction, valid in itself, between "true" and "false" practice of religion. The fact remains that in certain instances where religious attachment and practice have been entirely sincere, the individual finally emerges as a person strangely devoid of courage, morbidly attached to money, and hag-ridden by a thousand assorted fears.

You know, that centurion would have made a first-rate priest.

No Time to Waste

Then he rose up, and checked the winds, and the sea,
and there was deep calm. So that all asked in amazement:
What kind of man is this, who is obeyed even by the winds
and the sea? (Matthew 8:26–27; Gospel for the Fourth
Sunday after Epiphany)

On this day in this year, the glad liturgical cycle of
Christmas-Epiphany draws to a close. It can be useful,
at the conclusion of a liturgical season, to ask in what
precise way we have profited by another period of earnest
life in Christ. We may grant at once that incessant evalua-
tion of one's spiritual condition is no more to be advised
than preoccupation with one's physical well-being. The
present suggestion is merely that there may be a point in
occasionally taking one's temperature, whether of soul
or body.

As has been said so often, one purpose that underlies
the Church's liturgy and therefore the Church's calendar
is pedagogic. Primarily, of course, each Sunday Mother
Church calls her children together in order to offer to God
our Lord the communal Eucharistic worship, which
repeats again in mystery form the life, passion, death and
glorification of the Lord Christ and, indeed, the entire
history of men's salvation. The Bride of Christ hopes,

moreover, that the participation of her children in the
Eucharistic sacrifice will be complete; that they will par-
take (to use the language of this day's Post-communion)
of that *heavenly nourishment* which enables a man to
relish without harm his *earthly satisfactions.*

Yet always, in her mode of worship, our good Mother
Church has another end in mind. Her children of whatever age and learning and experience are still her children; and children need to be taught.

The lessons that the liturgy teaches would be very
difficult to enumerate. Consider the suggestions of our
present Mass text: in the entrance song, the propriety of
offering joyful praise to God; in the Epistle, the supreme
Christian law of love; in the Gospel, the vital truth that
we can never have too much faith and trust in Christ; in
two prayers, the gentle reminder of our *fragilitas,* our
instability, so that we will not presume. It is no objection
to say that all this is long since familiar to the Christian
mind. As every one of us knows perfectly well, profound
lessons of this kind are learned but slowly. So many of us
are perhaps less evil than spiritually heedless.

There is a further reason for the unremitting, prayerful
pedagogy of the Church. Each time we encounter the
liturgy of a particular Sunday or festival, we are not
exactly the persons we were at last encounter. With the
end of the Christmas-Epiphany season, we are now one
year older than last time. A shade richer in experience, we
might even be a little wiser and therefore more receptive
to wisdom. Unfailingly and as graciously as ever, the
Church speaks to us again. Now she secretly looks for a
better hearing.

It is useless to pretend that we are not sharply aware of one other aspect of liturgical pedagogy. Each one of us is allotted just so much class time in the school of Mother Church. On this final Sunday after Epiphany, we have used up a whole year of learning time since the last final Sunday after Epiphany. Really, there is no time to waste. There will be no extra tutoring in order to learn Christ before we meet Christ.

A Festival of Two

And [Simeon] said, blessing God: . . . This is the light which shall give revelation to the Gentiles, this is the glory of your people, Israel. (Luke 2:29, 32; Gospel of the Feast of the Purification)

Observed in Jerusalem in the fourth century, the liturgical celebration of the 40th day after the birth of Christ came into universal use in the sixth century. Is the occasion a festival of Mary or of Christ? Both, really. It is the feast of our Lady's Purification, and it is Candlemas—the ritual recognition of Christ the Light.

As they are set down in the first two chapters of the Lucan Gospel, the initial events involving John the Baptizer and the Lord Christ begin in the temple of Jerusalem, and they end there; three different scenes are laid in the temple. Surely the author of those chapters was writing with full recollection of the Old Testament prophet known as Malachi: *Look, I am going to send my messenger to prepare a way before me. And the Lord you are seeking will suddenly enter his temple; and the angel of the covenant whom you are longing for, yes, he is coming, says Yahweh Sabaoth. Who will be able to resist the day of his coming?*

Despite occasional prophetic utterances about its ultimate disappearance, the temple of Jerusalem is portrayed in the Old Testament as an object of the highest veneration. As the seat and symbol of God's living presence, the temple was utterly sacred. Non-Jews were permitted to enter only the outermost court of the immense building, and an irreverent word concerning the temple was a serious crime. The only specific charge (as far as our knowledge goes) brought against Christ in His trial before the Sanhedrin was that He had made a veiled threat against the temple. St. Paul, accused before the procurator Festus, offers a triple defense: *I have committed no crime against the Jewish law, or against the temple, or against Caesar.*

The sacred inviolability of the temple involved not only the idea of God's presence, but even more especially the idea (living and strong in our own day) of the final vindication and triumph of the Jewish nation. To the temple, in the time of the messianic fulfillment, "all peoples [will] resort for instruction and the word of Yahweh. The temple will be a house of prayer for all peoples, who will bring their wealth for its service." Thus biblical scholar Fr. John McKenzie.

The point, therefore, of the insistent temple theme in

Luke 1 and 2 is the actual fulfillment of Jewish hopes, exactly according to the prophecy of Malachi: *And the Lord you are seeking will suddenly enter his temple. Suddenly:* consider the reaction, as described, of old Simeon. So, the messianic age has dawned. Jesus of Nazareth is the expected One. We may note also that Simeon speaks of the Child both as *the light which shall give revelation to the Gentiles,* and as *the glory of your people, Israel.* In the Old Testament, *glory* was a mark of the saving presence of Yahweh.

There can be no doubt that the author of Luke 1 and 2 also meant to give prominence, in this episode, to the Mother of the Saviour, especially since the immediately following narrative is that of the finding in the temple. Simeon blesses both Mary and Joseph, but speaks only to Mary; and his solemn prophecy addressed to Mary concerns not only *this child,* but also *your own soul.*

It is always comforting when the liturgy, which is acted and worshiping theology, brings together, for our prayer and our joy, Jesus the Saviour and Mary His Mother, Christ the light of the world and Mary "our life, our sweetness and our hope."

That Problem Again

You know well enough that when men run in a race, the race is for all, but the prize for one; run, then, for victory. (1 Corinthians 9:24; Epistle of Septuagesima Sunday)

The liturgical color violet announces the approach of the Christian season of reflection and restraint, which culminates in the annual remembrance of Christ's passion and death. We would like to devote the three pre-Lenten Sundays to some discussion of a major, perennial Christian problem. We wish to consider the question of prayer.

Remember the catechism definition of prayer, the pat definition we learned as children? "Prayer is the lifting of the mind and heart to God." As children, we saw no special difficulty. We learned our prayers and said them. It never occurred to us that lifting is apt to be laborious. We had no way of knowing a large and broad truth: that prayer is a matter of serious concern to religious man. "Religious man" here means neither the professional religious nor the man of uncommon piety. It means any man of faith in God, and particularly the Christian.

The committed Christian knows well that he ought to pray. He could name the reasons. Because of God's honor, which is acknowledged in prayer. Because of man's sore need, which is poured out in prayer. Because of Christ's precept and example. Our Lord prayed, and bade us do as much. *This, then, is to be your prayer, Our Father* . . .

Moreover, the man of faith has no antecedent objection to prayer. Many a good fellow is painfully reticent on the whole subject of prayer and piety, but anyone who imagines that men object to praying has never seen ordinary men on a weekend retreat. What the honest Christian says about prayer constitutes not a complaint, but a humble admission: "I'm just not very good at it." What he means and would say, except that he supposes the professionals *are* good at it, is: prayer is necessary— but difficult.

He is right. He is right, and couldn't be more right, on both counts.

There are evident reasons why prayer is not easy. First, because any voluntary attention is demanding. We all love television precisely because it demands nothing of us. (Even so, in the middle of a heart-rending melodrama the poor, numbed mind is apt to wander feebly.) Second, because an apparently one-sided conversation is never easy. In prayer we speak to the invisible, silent and, as it so often seems, distant God. The process can be disheartening. Third, because prayer for the Christian is supposed to be more than an occasional thing; and it is very difficult to persevere faithfully with what involves effort.

So religious man turns, rightly, to his religious mentors and honestly pleads: "I know I ought to pray. I want to pray. I can't, really. Please, have you any suggestions?"

Such an artless and sincere request (if addressed to God, it would be first-rate prayer) deserves not only respect, but a serious, equally honest answer. For the present, however, let a further word be added concerning the difficulty of prayer.

If prayer were perfectly natural in the sense of being perfectly easy, there would have been little point in Christ's repeated imperatives on the subject. Imperatives are given when imperatives are needed. *Love your enemies, do good to those who hate you, pray for those who persecute and insult you*—such lofty commands make sense precisely as commands.

On the other hand, Christ does not issue orders for the performance of the impossible. When, in the sorrowful garden, Christ said to His sleepy friends, *Watch and pray,* they could have done it. They should have done it. He did.

The New Prayer

And the grain that fell in good soil stands for those who hear the word, and hold by it with a noble and generous heart, and endure, and yield a harvest. (Luke 8:15; Gospel of Sexagesima Sunday)

Slender, doubtless, seems the connection between this Lucan text and our present subject of prayer. Yet the scriptural verse might, as an adaptation, be read as a directive on prayer: *hold by it with a noble and generous heart, and endure, and yield a harvest.*

Like everything else of consequence in the Church and in Christian life, the question of converse with God is currently being broadly re-examined. In the quasi-petrification that took place in the Western religious world of the last 400 years, it is unlikely that Christian prayer would have escaped all chilling influence. It need not be fancied that few or none have prayed well in some four centuries, but responsible people now justly inquire whether the Christian of 1967 ought to pray in the manner of the Christian of 1567—and, indeed, whether he can. That every man must address himself to God in prayer, no one doubts. *How* contemporary man ought to pray, by what means or procedures he will pray to best advantage—that is the question.

A characteristic of the religious era just passed is said to have been a pronounced individualism. Each Christian man stood solitary, in some sort, before his God. A man's personal salvation was his primary and preoccupying concern. He was urged simply to turn his back on whatever tended in any fashion to compromise that personal salvation; he received his sacraments and said his prayers; he anticipated a strictly private judgment, on the basis of his individual performance, immediately after his death.

Clearly, there was nothing terribly wrong or violently unorthodox in this whole posture. One wonders only whether it was a balanced posture, whether it was the most truly Christian posture.

Certainly, as far as prayer was concerned, the emphasis was on private, personal dealings with God. Even at liturgical worship, each person in his devotions followed his individual inclination. At Mass, the parish church was wonderfully quiet.

Two other characteristics of recent Christian prayer may be mentioned briefly. Nonliturgical devotions, especially those connected with the saints, flourished. No prayer book was complete without a litany of litanies, a catalogue of petitionary prayers arranged for each day of the week, for three successive days, for nine days, for 30 days, and individual prayers addressed to a galaxy of little-known saints. This was the era of the three-day novena.

Finally, for those interested in or committed to the practice of mental prayer, there was a detailed "method" to be learned and heroically employed. Since the method enjoyed the highest credentials, no one had the hardihood to suggest that for many an earnest practitioner it didn't seem to work.

Without injustice to the sincere and often admirable—and sometimes very effective—prayer of yesterday, the Christian and especially the Catholic of the present may rejoice that contemporary emphases in the matter of prayer give him an advantage. Broadly speaking, individualist prayer is out; communal prayer is in. Nonliturgical devotions are out; liturgical, scriptural prayer is in. Mechanical method in speaking with God is out, spontaneity and freedom and artlessness are in.

A pair of mild cautions may now be introduced. One: the new prayer (which is not without its own problems) is meant to balance, not supplant, the old. Two: the new prayer may be easier. It is not easy.

A Primer of Prayer

Then Jesus stopped, and gave orders that the man should be brought to him; and when he came close, he asked him: What would you have me do for you? Lord, he said, give me back my sight. Jesus said to him: Receive your sight; your faith has brought you recovery. (Luke 18:40–42; Gospel of Quinquagesima Sunday)

On this last pre-Lenten Sunday, when the liturgical Gospel presents us with a splendid example of authentic prayer, it will not be out of place to offer some suggestions on the problem of prayer.

The success of any enterprise will depend primarily on the interior attitude with which one approaches the enterprise. Let a man turn to prayer in fundamental misunderstanding of what he is about, and there must follow disillusionment, disappointment and even disgust. Much is being said and written currently about the Christian "experience," and much that is being said and written is entirely sound. In distinction to the Protestant intuition, the Catholic has been reared in suspicion of religion as an experience and especially as an emotional experience. Such Catholic wariness could and did end, not seldom, in mechanistic dealing with God. The exaggeration is now being curbed; and now, ironically, the old warning must be honestly repeated in a limited way.

Above and before every other consideration in this
weighty matter, prayer must be regarded not as therapy,
not as satisfaction, not as a panacea, but as a service
rendered to God. In short, prayer is not what you get, but
what you give. The man of faith (significant description)
must pray, he must pray often, he must pray regularly.
Inclination has nothing to do with the issue, and neither
has success. Anyone who prays only when he feels like it,
or enjoys it, is certain to pray less . . . and less . . . and
less. It figures. As we remarked earlier on, lifting anything,
even the mind and heart to God, is hard work.

If there must be a choice, very well, it is better to pray
less in order to pray better—always provided we do not
finally, in stern logic, cease praying in order to pray perfectly. The principle applies particularly to prayers as distinct from prayer. The prolonged repetition of a strict
formula cannot but grow wearisome. Words can be repeated indefinitely, but with each repetition there is apt to
be less "presence" of the speaker in the words. Commercial
formulas are taped in order to prevent nervous break-
downs. It is of genuine interest that in the Sermon on the
Mount our Saviour, the supreme authority on prayer, is
recorded thus: *When you are at prayer, do not use many
phrases, like the heathens.* Observe the very real prayer in
this day's gospel: *Lord, he said, give me back my sight.*
The petition could scarcely be more brief. It could not be
more heartfelt.

Perhaps the major and certainly the primary effort in
all prayer must be some present recognition, some sense,
some realization, of that Other to whom we are speaking.
Such apperception is a subtle and even delicate business.

The question is not one of emotional response to the presence of God, nor is it at all necessary to visualize God with a white beard or Christ in a flowing robe. (The Holy Spirit has always been a problem in this regard.) The task is simply to *know*, to know strongly and quietly, that He to whom I speak is here, is attentive, is all love.

Prayer can be and often is experienced as an emptiness. Want to know what is in that emptiness? God.

The First and Last Truth

And now, to further that work [peace with God], we entreat you not to offer God's grace an ineffectual welcome. (2 Corinthians 6:1; Epistle of the First Sunday of Lent)

For reasons that have been accumulating over some little time, we propose to devote these lines, during the first four weeks of Lent, to a single subject. That subject is salvation as it is understood in the religious and especially the Christian sense.

We begin with a provided datum: the fact of personal immortality. Instantly the first question appears. Is immortality a fact?

Life after death is not a scientific fact. The supposition or contention of personal existence after death does not belong to an order of reality where scientific demonstra-

tion is possible. Moreover, one grows profoundly thoughtful as he reflects on the total absence of absolutely verifi-
able evidence from beyond the grave. Hamlet may be
blamed for his indecision; he certainly blames himself; yet
he is only being reasonable when he doubts the authenticity of his communication from another world. If he had
been schooled in depth psychology, hallucinatory com-
pensation and the death wish, he would have been even
more skeptical.

Personal immortality is an article of Christian belief. "I
believe in . . . the resurrection of the body, and life everlasting." (A human body, so like other human bodies, is
yet unique. It is the body of *this* person, and of no other.)
It is difficult to see how these linked propositions can
be strictly proved to one who does not accept them. The
Christian believes them.

The Christian endorses a further truth about immortality. He believes, on the strength of what appears to
him to be the lucid, unequivocal teaching of Christ, that
there are two mutually exclusive states of personal immortality. One is a state of supreme happiness. One is a
state of total misery. The professed follower of Christ ac-
cepts that either but not both of these conditions will be
his for all eternity.

It follows that the question of salvation is the paramount issue in the individual Christian life. It does not
follow that personal salvation is the only issue in the
Christian life. It does not follow that one's own salvation
is a value that exists and prevails in isolation from all
other values—for example, the well-being and ultimate
salvation of everyone else. The truth at stake here is

simple, and has been simply and authoritatively expressed: *How is a man the better for it, if he gains the whole world at the cost of losing his own soul?*

When men believe strongly in the primacy of eternal salvation, a danger arises that they may so magnify the notion of another and especially a better world that they will altogether denigrate the values of the present world in which they (and others) live. That such a heavy-handed emphasis on eternity and consequent slighting of the urgent here and now did actually take place in the propagation of the religion of Christ, no one will trouble to deny.

That such neglect of immediate reality produced certain regrettable results is likewise a matter of record. But that Christianity therefore is not and should not be essentially otherworldly is false. *My words,* said Christ truly of such sayings as we have but now quoted, *will stand.*

The Mystery of Salvation

We gave you a pattern of how you ought to live so as to please God . . . What God asks of you is that you should sanctify yourselves, and keep clear of fornication . . . For all such wrong-doing God exacts punishment; we have told you so already, in solemn warning. (1 Thessalonians 4:1, 3 and 6; Epistle of the Second Sunday of Lent)

In the present religious climate, which in so many ways is salubrious, it becomes necessary to insist that when a Christian shows concern for his eternal salvation, he neither dismisses the legitimate values of the here and now nor implies indifference to the welfare, whether immediate or ultimate, of everyone else. A Christian may indeed brood excessively on his eternal destiny, just as any person who lacks interior balance may grow neurotic and obsessive on any subject—money, for example. But the man who believes in what the Acts of the Apostles calls *the Way*—the way of life, with its ideals, motives and goals, shown by Christ—will not be faulted if he periodically reflects on the issue of salvation and, more practically, on the question of how salvation is to be achieved.

Eternal happiness is the fruit of teamwork, of knowing cooperation. Into the work enter both the grace of God and the willing effort of the individual.

The first observation to be made about the truth here expressed is a candid declaration of nescience. That God's grace and man's effort are related in the attainment of salvation, we know. *How* they are related, we do not exactly know.

Surely it will be clear to the man of faith that mystery must be accepted as an intrinsic element of revealed religion, and that mystery does not at all constitute a disabling factor in religion. If science is stimulated and not embarrassed by its manifold mysteries, why should not the man of faith be actually enlightened by supernatural truth whose total meaning he can never grasp? As was said long ago, the God who could be completely gotten inside the human head would not be much of a God. Besides, it must ever be repeated that in Christian mysteries of the practical order, such as this of attaining everlasting happiness, the believer understands amply enough for his needs. He knows that grace can be trusted, but without sloth. He knows that effort must be made, but without illusion. In short, for the supreme purpose of possessing God forever, the Christian knows (and it is much to know) what to do.

As the follower of Christ undertakes to operate, for his salvation, with the grace of Christ, he is aware that his situation involves two presuppositions and two problems.

The first presupposition is that man is substantially free to make choices. Depth psychology has rightly warned against illusory glibness in measuring interior human freedom at a moment and in a context. Nevertheless, it remains a most sharp human awareness that a person does make personal choices; that he chooses A when he might have chosen B or C; that he frequently chooses A with clear knowledge of the responsibility and consequences involved. The second presupposition is that a man's free choices exercise an influence on his final destiny. The Christian believes in God and in his own dignity in freedom as opposed to blind fate and mere mechanics.

The two salvation problems are, of course, presumption and Pelagianism. (Pelagius, a fourth-century British monk and optimist, is very much in evidence, these days.) Presumption means what it says: the individual need do nothing toward his salvation; God will do all. Pelagianism means that the whole job can be done and must be done by the individual. A man wills and sweats his way into the kingdom of heaven. Briefly, in the supreme work of salvation the man of presumption is unemployed. The Pelagian is self-employed.

The true Christian cries: *Lord, have mercy.* Then he is up and doing.

The Faithful One

At this time, Jesus had just cast out a devil, which was dumb; and no sooner had the devil gone out than the dumb man found speech. The multitudes were filled with amazement. (Luke 11:14; Gospel of the Third Sunday of Lent)

When we read or hear this crisp account of an act of the Lord Christ that instantly brought healing and wholeness —a token salvation—to a grievously handicapped man, we may almost unconsciously begin to suppose that final salvation will ensue from just such a direct and efficacious act on the part of almighty God, the individual remaining simply passive or, at most, eliciting at some time or other a vague act of faith. We may note, therefore, that this Lucan passage follows hard upon another in which our Saviour insists on the necessity of personal prayer. *Everyone that asks will receive, that seeks, will find, that knocks, will have the door opened to him.* Indeed the man of faith *will receive . . . will find . . . will have the door opened to him;* when he *asks . . . seeks . . . knocks.*

Thus we find fresh scriptural basis (to say nothing of this day's liturgical Epistle) for the teaching that eternal salvation finally results from a cooperation: a free co-operation of man with the freely given grace of God. But what we wish to notice now is God's part in the work of salvation. Whatever be its innermost nature, grace is a divine assistance freely and amply given to man. Such assistance is necessary for man. It is efficacious. It is available.

A dominant Old Testament theme that is taken up and strongly rehearsed by St. Paul, especially in the letter to the Romans, is the notion of God's fidelity. No single idea was more prominent in Jewish thought than that of a binding covenant between Israel and Israel's God. Israel was Yahweh's chosen, His beloved; and in the desert Israel had gratefully acknowledged this predilection and in turn had bound itself to Yahweh. The covenant was solemn, sacred and forever. It remained for the parties to be faithful to the holy pact.

There follows the prophetic cry—always sad, sometimes bitter—that rings again and again in the Old Testament; the cry that is heard so often and in varied forms on the lips of Christ Himself. Israel has been false to its word; God has been utterly faithful. God is true. He pledges, and He performs. Man may fail God, but God will not fail man.

It is very much more than rhetorical to say that we stand now at a moment in salvation history when we most urgently need to recall the loving fidelity of God. Whether there be question of the eternal salvation of this individual—of this *me!*—or of the security and well-being of men as they are led and taught by the Church, we need to be convinced anew that God in His power and wisdom and mercy will not fail us. Men of faith will debate increasingly what is meant by the very terms *faith, faithful, fidelity,* but God our Lord will neither wonder nor wander nor waver in His faithfulness to mankind and to each man. We may be astonished at the ways in which grace works. We may even hesitate in our description of what grace is. But the grace will be there. God has given us our beginning; He has appointed our end. He has pledged to see us from the one to the other. He will do so.

God is faithful. Now, about you and me . . .

Means to the End

And Jesus took the loaves, and gave thanks, and distributed them to the company, and a share of the fishes, too, as much as they had a mind for. (John 6:11; Gospel of Laetare Sunday)

Man's salvation is the outcome of cooperation between man's sincere effort and God's abundant and powerful grace. How does man come by the grace of God?

The first and simplest answer to this practical question has been provided by Christ Himself: *Ask, and the gift will come; seek, and you shall find; knock, and the door shall be opened to you. Everyone that asks, will receive, that seeks, will find, that knocks, will have the door opened to him.* (This saying must have been familiar to the early Christians. It is recorded in identical terms by both Matthew and Luke.) The most immediate means to grace, and thus to salvation, is prayer.

Normal people are normally reticent on the subject of their most personal dealings with almighty God; otherwise, it might be instructive to conduct, in the matter of prayer, one of those surveys that are meat and drink and headlines to us nowadays. The survey would consist of two questions only. One: What portion of your prayer is petitionary? Two: What portion of your petitionary prayer is addressed to spiritual rather than material assistance?

Let there be repeated the broad truth that the sight and possession of God forever stands quite beyond the order of objectives that can be achieved by strenuous effort alone. Unlike suitable weight, eternal happiness cannot be gained simply by tenacious dieting and exercise of one kind or another. Creation is a gift, and grace is a gift, and salvation is a gift. Moreover, one's physical creation belongs to the natural order, while grace and salvation belong to that supernatural economy where sheer, ethical effort has, in itself, no true currency.

So the Christian begs God (who, on His part, is more eager to answer this than any other prayer) for the needed assistance in order that—to employ a respected formula—

he may indeed "praise, reverence and serve God our Lord, and by this means save his soul." The anguished cry of Simon Peter, attempting to walk on the water, is entirely suitable for our regular and heartfelt use: *Then, seeing how strong the wind was, he lost courage and began to sink; whereupon he cried aloud, Lord, save me.*

A second means to grace is that which is symbolized in this day's liturgical Gospel: the Eucharist.

The pronounced human tendency, whether in alarm or eagerness, to oversimplify a complex or technical question and then state it in extreme form is being thoroughly exercised in the post-conciliar Church. A responsible spokesman will note the distinction between liturgical and non-liturgical prayer. Shortly we hear a feverish outcry that "nobody"—nobody, that is, in a right and Christian mind —is saying the rosary any more. Let a person of a certain stamp learn that somewhere, under some unknown conditions, a general absolution has been imparted, and that enthusiast begins to dance on what he identifies as the grave of auricular confession.

Here, precisely, is the possibly serious problem that currently arises in connection with the Eucharist. The altar of reposition is now distinguished, spatially, from the altar of sacrifice. Does it by any logic follow that the Catholic practice of praying, apart from liturgical celebration, before Christ in the Eucharist—the thoughtful, consoling, highly religious "visit" to the Blessed Sacrament—is now altogether démodé? Expert theologians carefully discuss the aptness of certain terms that have long been employed in explaining, so far as may be, the living presence of Christ in the Eucharist. Thereupon some Catholics reportedly begin to abstain—not now from meat on Friday, but from Holy Communion on Sunday.

Prayer and the sacraments, as means of grace and instruments of salvation, are here to say.

The Scandal and the Splendor

And now he grew sorrowful and dismayed; my soul, he said, is ready to die with sorrow. . . . And now he was in an agony, and prayed still more earnestly; his sweat fell to the ground like thick drops of blood. (Matthew 26:38 and Luke 22:43–44; from the Gospel narrative of the Passion)

The agony of the Lord Christ in the garden of Gethsemane is one of the supreme riddles of the Gospel witness. If the Gospels were fiction, this episode would never have been included. The mysterious event is mentioned, is described at some length in all its pathos and scandal—and is not in the least explained. Questioned, the evangelists (all but John recount the agony) might well have appeared troubled and uneasy; but they would have said stubbornly: "It is what happened." Those simple words must remain the basis, and very nearly the extent, of Christian reflection on the agony.

The Supper, that last and first of its sacred kind, had ended in all the tranquil exaltation of the Lord's high-priestly prayer. Christ is serene, sure, perfectly composed. Under the bright stars and in the flooding whiteness of the paschal moon, He leads the familiar way to Geth-semane. Suddenly: *And now he grew sorrowful and dis-mayed; my soul, he said, is ready to die with sorrow.* What has happened? No enemy is in sight, there seems nothing to fear. In the velvet night a distant dog barks and a quick wind stirs, but the peace of the garden is undisturbed. What has happened to the Saviour? As the frightening scene goes on, one wonders in a kind of panic if this un-manned man is the Christ he has known. The Son of Man —oh, that name!—he grows fiercely tense, He wallows in black depression, He seems wildly uncertain, He cries out in pleading, He is plainly and simply terrified. He cannot be still, but must beat a path from the shadowy place of His lonely suffering to where His closest friends lie sleep-ing, and we hear from His lips a cry of desperate need and sore disappointment in tones we have never heard before.

The fact, the sheer fact, is indeed the true meditation on the agony. The Saviour of the world, face to face with death—and with what other horrors, we know not—all but goes to pieces, before the eyes of watching men until the end of time. In the most exact sense of the ready phrase, it is too bad. The agony in the garden is a shame and a scandal.

Every effort, however sincere and devout, to analyze the agony must come to a dead end, must terminate in a blank wall. The man Christ did not, in His human nature, wish to be tortured and die. But men not a few have faced torture and death with steadiness. What, then? Did He, there under the olive trees, experience some total and totally shattering abandonment? If so, why? Is there place here for Paul's mysterious saying: *Christ never knew sin, and God made him into sin for us, so that in him we might be turned into the holiness of God?* If so, what does this mean?

What is certain is that the Lord Christ is never more human, never more truly one of us, than in that long agony in Gethsemane. His anguish, like so much of ours, is within Him. He lies soaked in an abnormal sweat; but what is bleeding is His heart. And as every one of us must do more often than we say, He suffers quite alone. Trembling, He reaches out for human help. There is none.

Two other facts matter. Christ, being *in an agony . . . prayed still more earnestly*. The other fact: Christ triumphed at last over His sore distress. Torches begin to flicker in the darkness, harsh whispers are heard, there is the clink of armor. Turning, His shoulders lifted, the Saviour walks steadily and calmly to treachery and death.

Notes on a Death

At last they had done with mockery; stripping him of the scarlet cloak, they put his own garments on him, and led him away to be crucified. . . . Here they offered him a draught of wine, mixed with gall, which he tasted but

would not drink, and then crucified him. (Matthew 27:31
and 34–35; from the Passion narrative)

The Lord Jesus is abandoned by His friends before He is
rejected by His enemies. "With friends like these, who
needs enemies?" The avowed followers of Christ sometimes show little of the resourcefulness, determination and
wholeheartedness of those who dislike and would be rid
of Him.

*   *   *

" 'There is no need for a Messiah such as this Jesus from
Nazareth—there cannot even be such a Messiah!' Thus,
Jesus is condemned in the name of good order, national
pride, the good of the country, truth, belief in Yahweh,
theology and philsophy, beauty and symmetry—really in
the name of everything [decent] on the face of the earth."
(K. Rahner)
     Men should always be afraid, and most of all if they are
proceeding to unusual or severe measures, when they are
utterly, absolutely certain that they are right.

*   *   *

It is of paramount importance to grasp the exact reason
for the Sanhedrin's condemnation of Christ. The determining question of Caiphas—*I adjure thee by the living
God to tell us whether thou art the Christ, the Son of
God*—must be linked with the final and finally true charge
laid before Pilate: *He ought to die, for pretending to be
the Son of God.* Every Israelite was a son of God; hence

the accusation, like the question of Caiphas, must be understood in its most exalted, metaphysical and shocking sense. If *this* divine claim is false, then justly, if not in due legal form, was He crucified. In every way the crucifix calls for the supreme act of faith in Jesus.

*   *   *

Christ in prison must be the comfort and support of all of us, imprisoned as we are in our personal destiny, in the absurdity of this individual temperament, in our life-long disappointments, in our unimpeachable sentence to death.

*   *   *

Concerning Pilate: "In God's eyes, what ultimately counts is not an intellect that is pleasingly skeptical and coolly calculating. What He wants is a simplicity and a total dedication that come out for Him alone, and we must not try to avoid His love by opting for something apparently better." (K. Rahner)

The Roman governor is the polite sophisticate, securely armored in his charming skepticism. It is astonishing how quickly and completely his defenses are riddled. When we last see him, he is a cowed, spiritless, judicial murderer. Skepticism is a poor substitute for moral courage, and sophistication may fall far short of wisdom.

*   *   *

The scourging, crowning with thorns: The savage attack upon the body of Christ reminds us that the human body

—and *that* body!—and the human spirit form one essential reality that is, in fact, everlasting. Christian thought should be given to the nobility of the body—how it can praise God our Lord by its purity, by its racking pains bravely borne, by its growing feebleness in age.

* * *

Jesus drank the vinegar, and said: It is achieved. Then he bowed his head and yielded up his spirit. So Christ did die. That death was not apparent, but real; as real as my death will be. So be it. If death was good enough for Him, it is good enough for me.

* * *

Ecce homo: See, here is the man. Yes, oh yes: look at Him, look at Him.

But Why the Passion?

He dispossessed himself, and took the nature of a slave, fashioned in the likeness of men, and presenting himself to us in human form; and then he lowered his own dignity, accepted an obedience which brought him to death, death on a cross. (Philippians 2:7–8; Epistle of Palm Sunday)

Of the special liturgical seasons in the Church Cardinal Newman wrote: "They are times when we may humbly expect a larger grace, because they invite us especially to the means of grace." Such a time is Passiontide: it invites us to that concerned reflection on the Lord Christ and His accepted destiny that is itself a grace. So we reverently note again the actual sufferings on Christ, we marvel at the incredible detachment of the Gospel narrative, we ponder the exalted identity of Him who suffers. Then the Christian presses on to other considerations.

What is the reason for Christ's passion and death? We know, of course, that Jesus of Nazareth, like many another bold, determined and outspoken innovator in human history, was done to death because He threatened and therefore outraged the established order in which He lived. The fact is instructive but of secondary importance. In the eternal designs of God, who, according to the conviction of men of faith, rules the universe and all history, what was the reason for the dreadful destiny of His Son?

Propter nos et propter nostram salutem. The words, neither arbitrary nor casual, are taken from the Christian credal declaration. *On account of us and on account of our salvation* the divine Son of God became man, suffered, died. (For our present purposes we omit mention of the resurrection, without which, however, the eternal plan stands incomplete.) The reason for the passion and death of our Lord is the final well-being of mankind.

If now it be asked: "But why did the economy of salvation involve such abasement and torment, such an appalling death, for God's Son?"—one finds himself recalling a passage in St. Paul, with its echoes of Isaiah: *How deep*

*is the mine of God's wisdom, of his knowledge; how in-
scrutable are his judgments, how undiscoverable his ways!
Who has ever understood the Lord's thoughts, or been his
counselor?*

This much may be said. Significantly, the salvation of
mankind was accomplished by the act of sacrifice, that
human action of giving and surrender which, beyond all
else that man can do, proclaims the sovereignty and good-
ness of God. The passion of Christ, which had for its
prologue the sacrificial paschal supper, constituted the
supreme and perfect act of worshiping, thankful, atoning,
pleading sacrifice to God. Such is the theme of the Epistle
to the Hebrews.

Familiar as it is, one further consideration in this
mystery of Christ's passion must not be overlooked. Suppose for a moment that the Gospel witness to Christ ended
with the splendid Transfiguration, or with the unqualified
triumph of this Palm Sunday, followed only by an exul-
tant ascension into heaven. Would such a plan of salvation, valid as it would have been, have made no difference
to the struggling, suffering follower of Christ? The question need but be asked to answer itself. Take away the
passion and death of Christ, and you take away the Christ
who has been the secret and the strength of countless
afflicted lives.

The history of mankind is, on one side, a story of racked
bodies and torn hearts and scalding tears. Sometimes, indeed, a desperate, despairing man will look down at the
fragments of his shattered existence and simply choose
death, with all its dark mystery, in preference to agonized
life. The believer in Christ, heartsore and crushed as he

may at some time be, will stand at the foot of a cross. He will look up, not down. He will be steadied, enlightened, strengthened, and at last quieted.

The Far Side of Death

And they went into the tomb, and saw there, on the right, a young man seated, wearing a white robe; and they were dismayed. But he said to them: No need to be dismayed; you have come to look for Jesus of Nazareth, who was crucified; he has risen again, he is not here. (Mark 16:5–6; Gospel of Easter Sunday)

What is on the other side of death? That bleak question has ever tormented mankind, and all the prodigious efforts to answer it through natural or psychic means have ended in failure. So each one of us, when the mood is on him, will reflect: "Some day—soon, maybe—I will close my eyes for the last time. Then what?"

Easter serves notice that what lies on the other side of death is life. That plain statement must not be glossed over or accepted routinely. Say it and think it again: On the far side of death is life. Immediately we must reject all those fanciful notions of a dream-like, ghostly pseudo-life with which literary imagination has made us familiar. The Christ of Easter is not a shade, but a live, breathing, speaking, touching, acting man. He appears; but He is not an apparition.

A detail in the Gospel of St. Luke is enormously important. *Then, while [the disciples] were still doubtful, and bewildered with joy, he asked them: Have you anything here to eat? So they put before him a piece of roast fish, and a honeycomb; and he took these and ate in their presence.* It makes a most pertinent Easter meditation to picture the risen, cheerful Saviour removing, with fingers sticky from the honeycomb, a small fish bone from His mouth. The life that the risen Christ demonstrates may be and is mysterious—there is so much we will not know about it until we have it—but it is what we understand and desire as life. Beyond the grave is not cessation, not darkness, not nothingness, not endless sleep, not colorless absorption into the uncaring universe, not some illusory mock-existence, but life: actual, literal life. Says the Lord Christ in the Johannine Gospel: *I am the resurrection and the life.*

Easter provides a further and equally deep comfort. The life that Christ shows us after death is the life of a person: a person in alert, happy, loving contact and union with other persons. Unquestionably, the most agonizing pain we experience in mortal life is the loss, by death, of those we most love. Surely also, a major factor in the stark fear of one's own death is the terrible loneliness of it. Alone, one passes into—aloneness? No, by no means, not at all, is the Easter answer to that dreadful question. Again, picture the risen Christ sitting easily among His beloved friends. In death a person painfully parts company with persons; and emerges, the identical person (however transformed), into the loving company of real persons: of Father, Son and Holy Spirit, of all those most dear to him who have gone before. Not idly does the liturgy speak of believers in Christ as a *familia,* a family. Easter promises a family reunion.

It is evident, lastly, that the Easter life is joyous. The risen Christ speaks no heavy word, encounters no enemy, is lifted above all controversy and conflict, shows no signs of tension or struggle, breathes calm and joy and peace. That calm and joy and peace He imparts. *He himself stood in the midst of them, and said, Peace be upon you; it is myself, do not be afraid.*

Reader and friend in Christ: at another Easter time lines very like these will be written and read, but not by you and not by me. Will we be dead? No. We will be living, together and content—God grant it—in Christ.

All Is Well

I have risen, and I am with you still. (Psalm 138:18; Entrance Song of the Easter Mass)

The literal resurrection of Jesus of Nazareth from literal death, at once both a fact of history and an object of faith, has a triple meaning for those who believe in it. The resurrection of Christ means life. It means victory. It means joy.

In each instance, the significance holds first for Christ
Himself, then for sincere adherents of Christ.

Of course, the resurrection of the Saviour immediately
demonstrates the reality of life after death. But such obvious inference is only the beginning of the truth that is
here contained. "The resurrection may be called the
supremely divine work, because it is strictly the divinization of man by the virtue of the spirit. It is not only a re-
animation, which would be merely a return to and a
prolonging of mortal life, even if that life were to be prolonged indefinitely. But it is the passing from one mode of
existence to another." Thus Fr. Jean Daniélou. The resurrection of our Lord pledges to the believer ultimate
entrance into a life so rich, so radiant, so radically exalted
and perfect, that it can indeed be called—all pantheistic
foolishness aside—*divinization*. With cunning beyond all
that is human, the tempter whispered to Eve: *You yourselves will be like gods*. He lied. The risen Christ might
use the same words to us—in very truth.

Christ our Lord encountered human foes in His mortal
life. He fought them with fierce determination and dev-
astating effect, but in the end they prevailed. High priest
Caiphas had said, shrugging his shoulders: *It is best for us
if [this] one man is put to death*. So Christ died the death
of the crucified, and was buried. *And on the third day he
rose again*. The Saviour triumphed over His mortal enemies; and He never once mentions them or bothers about
them again. Christ's victory is not local but cosmic.

What the risen Saviour has conquered is evil—pure
evil, cosmic evil. He has conquered it by nullifying forever
its supremely symbolic effect, death. He has conquered

it by the cleansing power of the blood He shed. It was on the evening of the resurrection day, remember, that Christ bestowed upon His Church for all time the divine power absolutely to forgive sin. What Christ bested in His coming from the tomb is the leering, ape-like reality that lurks behind all evil, that implacable fallen angel who will not give over his plan to poison all that is good, that invisible malice who, if he were capable of delight, would delight that so many men no longer believe in him. The resurrection says: "Evil can be beaten. Evil *is* beaten—by, in and with Christ."

Surely, then, the majestic bursting of the tomb prison on that far-off Sunday morning must mean joy to the Christian, as it meant joy to Christ. The Lord Christ, stout warrior that He was, did rejoice in His victory, and His joy appears characteristically: in His quiet, gentle, gracious serenity. It is impossible to listen to the risen Christ as He softly calls Magdalen by name; as He says to His scared disciples: *Peace be upon you;* as He asks the bumbling man who had so furiously denied Him: *Simon, son of John, do you care for me?*—it is impossible thus to observe this most wondrous and wonderful Conqueror, and remain a stranger to Christian joy.

Christ is risen. All is well.

The Singular Witness

Then he said to Thomas: Let me have your finger; see, here are my hands. Let me have your hand; put it into my side. Cease your doubting, and believe. Thomas answered: You are my Lord and my God. (John 20:27–28; Gospel of Low Sunday)

From this first Sunday after Easter until Pentecost—for a period, that is, of seven successive Sundays—the second of the liturgical readings (the Mass-Gospel) is taken from the Gospel of St. John. We will accept the broad hint of the liturgy. We undertake an unpretentious examination of the fourth, the last and most fascinating, volume of evangelical witness.

The most immediate observation to make about the fourth Gospel is that it is unique among the Gospels. Matthew, Mark and Luke are known traditionally as the Synoptics: granted variations (particularly in Luke) of the story they tell, they share a common point of view. The resemblances between them are as obvious as they are striking. John is different. John is so different that rationalist critics have subjected this Gospel to the most punishing and skeptical examination. They have questioned both the identity of the writer and the hstoricity of the writing; they have spoken of the Johannine work as "a novel about

Jesus of Nazareth." They have asked a large question: is the Christ of St. John really the Christ of the Synoptics?

What are some of the more evident differences between the fourth Gospel and the other three?

It would not be true to say that the action of the first three Gospels takes place in Galilee (northern, rustic Palestine), while the scene of the Johannine witness is Jerusalem (the sophisticated religious and political center of Judea in the south). Yet the statement touches upon a fact. Turn the pages of the Gospel of St. Mark. The opening scene, the baptism of Christ, is laid in the south. At once we read: *Jesus came into Galilee, preaching the gospel of God's kingdom.* Thereafter we encounter numerous references to place, and always the place lies in or around Galilee: Capharnaum, Decapolis, Tyre and Sidon. Twice we hear of *scribes who had come from Jerusalem* to hear Christ. In chapter 10 we read of a circuitous journey that finally takes the Saviour to Jerusalem; but there follows the account of Palm Sunday, when the Lord's mortal life had but five days to run.

Now turn the pages of the fourth Gospel. *So Jesus went up to Jerusalem,* we read in chapter 2, and John places the cleansing of the temple here. There is a return to Galilee in chapter 4, but at the beginning of 5 we have: *After this came a Jewish feast, for which Jesus went up to Jerusalem.* The stirring events of chapter 6 occur in Galilee. Early in chapter 7 the Saviour returns, unattended and quietly, to Jerusalem—and we hear of no further events in Galilee. There is, then, a decided difference in locale between John and the Synoptics.

Connected with the question of locale is John's repeated

—and chronologically troublesome—mention of Jewish festivals, as in chapters, 2, 5, 6, 7, 10 and 12. The feast days generally provide the reason for the Lord's coming to the Holy City. With the exception, of course, of the final Passover, we find no reference in the Synoptics to these festivals.

Another contrast between John and the other Evangelists is curious. A favorite pedagogical device employed by our Lord was the parable, the more or less detailed story of the fictional sort that conveys a clear moral lesson. The Synoptics are much concerned with the parables. Many and vivid samples are provided, and the inspired writers even make Christ's use of parables something of an issue. John has no parables. He speaks of Christ as *the good shepherd,* but this is an image, not a story-with-moral. It might be added that the special character of Christ's teaching as recorded by John extends far beyond the question of method. Of this matter, more later.

Teasing as they are, the Johannine variants we have mentioned would seem relatively superficial. The problem must be pursued. There need be no delay, however, in the gratitude we feel to the last Evangelist for the invaluable and special Christ-data that he, prompted by the Holy Spirit and out of his sharp remembrance and deep meditation, has provided for us.

The "Spiritual" Gospel

I am the good shepherd; my sheep are known to me and know me; just as I am known to the Father, and know him. (John 10:14–15; Gospel of the Second Sunday after Easter)

"Seeing that the Gospels set forth only the material story, John, the last of all, entreated by his familiar friends and divinely upheld by the Spirit, wrote the spiritual Gospel." Thus commented Clement of Alexandria at the very end of the second century after Christ. Clement's observation, which has been ceaselessly quoted, is a thundering over-simplification; but it is not false. Relatively, set beside the Synoptics, the fourth Gospel *is* the "spiritual Gospel."

The intention of St. John, in the words of Msgr. Lucien Cerfaux, is that we must "see the life of Christ as illuminated from within by the manifestation of the Word, who is Life and Light." "The Synoptics," he says, "are chiefly concerned with the history; the Gospel of John is written on the historical plane, but in such a way that the historical plane receives light projected from a higher plane, that of the manifestation of the Word." If we were to compete with old Clement in the way of merciless simplification, we might say that Matthew, Mark and Luke give us Gospels of straightforward fact. John gives us a Gospel of inner and subtle meaning.

The first and most emphatic indication of the special character of the fourth Gospel is, of course, its celebrated prologue. In the earlier Gospels there is nothing remotely like this prologue. Matthew begins with the earthly genealogy of Christ, Mark starts with John the Baptist, Luke with Zachary the priest; each Evangelist makes a beginning that is factual, that is firmly rooted in human history. John begins (to use the traditional expression) *in sinu Patris, in the bosom of the Father.* John's starting point in his witness to Christ is supra-temporal, extra-terrestrial, super-natural. Employing a Greek term— *Logos, the Word*—unused by the Synoptics, John, the supreme poet-prophet-seer, proclaims unequivocally the pre-existence and the divinity of the Word. John then identifies the Word, *the Father's only-begotten Son,* with Jesus Christ. Note that this overwhelming declaration is made not as the conclusion of the Johannine witness, but as its solemn exordium.

But the prologue is by no means the only indication of the "spiritual" quality of the fourth Gospel. It is instructive to compare the discourses of Christ as recorded by the Synoptics with the discourses of the Saviour in John. Again speaking broadly, what our Lord is talking about in the earlier Gospels is *the kingdom of heaven, the kingdom of God,* in its relation to men. What Christ talks about in John is Himself in relation to the Father. Here is a pertinent question for study by all who may be interested: In the Synoptics, how many *I am* . . . statements does the Lord make? But how many such statements does John put upon the Saviour's lips? Further, what is the nature and scope of those soaring declarations? As: *I am the light of*

the world. Or: *Before ever Abraham came to be, I am.*
Or: *I am the resurrection and life.* Or: *My Father and I
are one.* It is evident that John has small interest in "facts"
as distinct from meaning.

Another of the significant depths in the fourth Gospel
is the problem of determining precisely where, in a passage, the words of Christ end and the personal reflection of
John begins. Recall also that the entire 17th chapter
(though verse three may be an incorporated footnote) is
given over to the sublime utterance of the Saviour that is
known as the "sacerdotal prayer." Finally, consider that
this last evangelical witness is the Gospel of the Holy
Spirit. Take away John, and what is the sum of our
Gospel knowledge of the Third Person in God?

Let the important point be repeated. What John gives
us is neither doctored facts nor merely apparent facts. He
gives us facts-with-meaning; and clearly values the one
only for the other.

The Gospel of Encounter

*At this time Jesus said to his disciples: After a little while,
you will see me no longer, and again after a little while
you will have sight of me, because I am going back to the
Father.* (John 16:16; Gospel of the Third Sunday after
Easter)

There is in the fourth and last of the Gospels a certain
unobtrusive insistence that finds a distinct echo in the
opening verses of the canonical First Epistle of St. John.
The note is first struck in the words that follow the cli-
mactic pronouncement—*And the Word was made flesh,
and came to dwell among us*—of the exalted Prologue to
the Gospel. The words are: *and we had sight of his glory.*
In this brief statement stress is undoubtedly laid upon
what was seen; but there is emphasis also on the sheer fact
that the Incarnate Word was actually seen.

Turn, now, to the Gospel's second chapter and the
story of the water-into-wine miracle, where the abundance
of intimate detail suggests an eyewitness account. We read:
*So, in Cana of Galilee, Jesus began his miracles, and made
known the glory that was his*—presumably to and through
eyewitnesses. In chapter 19, after the vivid description of
the lancing of the side of Christ as He hung in death on
the cross, we have this abrupt statement from the Gospel's
author: *He who saw it has borne witness; and his witness
is worthy of trust.* An equivalent declaration is made in
the final verses of the entire Gospel.

Here are the opening verses of John's First Epistle:
*Our message concerns that Word who is life; what he was
from the first, what we have heard about him, what our
own eyes have seen of him; what it was that met our gaze,
and the touch of our hands. Yes, life dawned; and it is as
eyewitnesses that we give you news of that life, that eternal
life, which ever abode with the Father and has dawned,
now, on us. This message about what we have seen and
heard we pass on to you, so that you too may share in our
fellowship.*

The Johannine witness constitutes a Gospel of personal experience of Christ, the Word made flesh.

One of the aspects of the present religious ferment in the Christian world is the determined revolt against the legalistic the formalistic, the mechanistic, in religion. Youth, in particular, fiercely rejects all that appears "phony," both in life and in religious tradition. The cry is for "meaningful" religion, for some kind of direct, immediate experience of the holy. One realizes, of course, that the possibility of destructive illusion cannot be ruled out of this current religious stance or mood. Nevertheless, warning must not be the last word here. Received Christian and especially Catholic postures and procedures had in truth grown stiff and in some sort mechanical. External observance may always tend to take the place of inner conviction and personal attachment. It is always possible that the letter of the law will acquire an ascendency over the spirit of the law.

So, then, the present quest for personal experience of authentic religious reality is by no means merely petulant or emotive. But the remarkable fact is that personal experience of Christ is precisely what John in his Gospel is recording; it is exactly what John wishes his readers to share. Anyone who will perceptively read the fourth Gospel will become gradually aware of a certain tone, a certain texture, a certain strong impression, that is not nearly so noticeable in the Synoptics. The reader of St. John finds himself not only amazingly close to the events recorded, but actually in warm, close, clear relationship to the august Person of whom John says: *We had sight of his glory.*

If, with John and with some measure of John's simplicity and freshness, we look at and experience the Christ of the fourth Gospel, we too will in our degree catch *sight of his glory.*

The Gospel of Signs

I have still much to say to you, but it is beyond your reach as yet. It will be for him, the truth-giving Spirit, when he comes, to guide you into all truth. (John 16:12–13; Gospel of the Fourth Sunday after Easter)

Again and again it is necessary to warn against violent simplifications as we note the special quality of the last of the four Gospels. When we observe that the Gospel of St. John is theological, is spiritual, is a gospel of meaning, there is not the faintest suggestion that the Synoptic Gospels are not profoundly theological, deeply spiritual, replete with implicit meaning. When we say that the Synoptics, and especially Mark, are more strictly factual and historical, we do not for an instant hint that the fourth Gospel is poetry or allegory rather than history. The point simply is that John, who is very like Matthew, Mark and Luke, is very different from them.

Consider, for example, the element of miracle in the Synoptics and in John. The first three Gospels abound in miraculous happening brought about by our Lord. The

miracles are of every variety, from instantaneous cures of
desperate illness to the landing of a fish with a tax-payment
in its mouth, and upon occasion the wonders are so numerous that they are reported compendiously. Moreover, al-
though the Synoptics regularly establish a connection between a miracle and faith, they do not concern themselves
with reading a meaning into a miraculous event. Inci-
dentally, it is most interesting to note that the Transfiguration of Christ, which John does not mention, is
recounted by the other three Evangelists in the same
general way. They describe the unique happening, and
make no attempt to explain it.

St. John's word for miracle is *sign*. The point about any
true sign is that it does not exist in its own right and for
its own sake. It exists for the purpose of signifying. How
many "signs" does John narrate? Seven; and since seven,
like three and twelve and forty, is a favored biblical number, there is at once a suggestion of particular significance
underlying the surface chronicle. What is more, in five of
the seven cases (with corresponding hints in the other two)
the sign is immediately connected with a discourse that
interprets the sign and reads its theological meaning.

In John 2 we have the story of the water-into-wine wonder at Cana. The meaning: Christ makes the difference
between the Old and the New Dispensation. John 4 gives
us what the author calls *the second sign,* the healing of an
official's son. The meaning: Faith is the one requisite. The
cure of a cripple occurs in chapter five. Meaning: Christ
is our true health. Chapter 6 has two signs: the feeding of
the multitude (Christ our food) and the walking on the
water (Christ our safe guide). We encounter unusually

circumstantial sign-narratives in chapters 9 and 11: the healing of a man born blind (Christ our light) and the raising of Lazarus (Christ our life). Particular significance attaches to the last two signs, since the evident twin theme of the Johannine Gospel is light and life.

Clearly, for St. John, a miracle is exactly as described in an old formula: a wonder with a meaning in it. What is more, John is manifestly more interested in the meaning than in the wonder. Is it likely, then, that in his narrative John has reshaped, for his theological purpose, the received story of a miracle performed by Christ? It is likely. Does it follow that John's sign-stories are essentially devout fiction? It does not follow. Setting aside details, all of John's miracles except the first have parallels in the Synoptics. Also, and for what it is worth, a certain eyewitness impression is undeniably made by the narratives of the fourth Gospel.

A sign signifies. The supreme sign of the Johannine Gospel is the Johannine Gospel.

The Gospel of the Only-Begotten Son

Now comes the hour when I will talk to you in parables no longer, but tell you openly about the Father. . . . It was from the Father I came out, when I entered the world, and now I am leaving the world, and going on my way to the Father. (John 16:25, 28; Gospel of the Fifth Sunday after Easter)

In speaking of Jesus of Nazareth as the Son of God, the New Testament on just five occasions adds to the title the adjective *only-begotten.* All occurrences of the qualifying term are found in the canonical writings attributed to John Barzebedee. Without making an issue of a single term—which, however, was early embodied in the Christian Creed—we may note its double force. It says sonship. It says uniqueness. It is another indication of what the author of the fourth Gospel declares so explicity and so insistently: that the Jesus whom he knew and saw and heard and touched is not only the long awaited Messias, but the natural and thus divine Son of God.

Whatever be the ultimate findings of responsible scholarship with regard to the authorship, structure and strata of the fourth Gospel, the book as we have it stands as the supreme evangelical witness to the literal divinity of Christ. From beginning to end, from the explicit pronouncement of the Prologue to the explicit confession of Thomas the doubter, the Johannine Gospel proclaims Jesus as the only-begotten Son of God. Certain statements placed on the lips of Christ in this Gospel could hardly be more undisguised: *My Father and I are one. . . . The Father is in me, and I in the Father. . . . Anyone who has seen me has seen the Father.*

It is always possible, of course (and advisable, too), to question the exact weight of particular expressions used by an author who speaks to us from a remote culture. What makes the Johannine witness to Christ so decisive is John's reiterated declaration of the plain purpose of his Gospel: *that you may learn to believe Jesus is the Christ, the Son of God, and so believing find life in his name.* Even more than the Synoptics, the last proclamation of the good news of Christ is a summons to faith. Simply as an item for the record, the verb meaning "to believe" is used, by Matthew, Mark and Luke together, 34 times. It is used by John 98 times.

Notice must be taken of a further aspect of the fourth Gospel as a gospel of faith. The consequence of belief in Jesus as *the Christ, the Son of God,* is that the believer will *find life in his name.* The future tense in this context, however, belies the Johannine thought. Such faith in Jesus means life immediately, here and now. That life is obviously of a supernatural order, it is emphatically declared to be eternal; but it begins, it is, it is possessed, *now.*

There follows a certain grave conclusion with regard to the fourth Gospel, a conclusion that is not straightway evident in the lofty tone and in the appealing imagery and in the consoling dicta of the book. The witness of John is a gospel of judgment. The man who refuses faith in Christ as *the Son of God* stands forthwith self-condemned. There is no true *life* in him or for him. *When God sent his Son into the world, it was not to reject the world, but so that the world might find salvation through him. For the man who believes in him, there is no rejection; the man who does not believe is already rejected; he has not found faith in the name of God's only-begotten Son.*

The Gospel of St. John is many things: a sublime utterance; an unforgettable vision; a trumpet call; a warmth laid to the heart; a most grave and solemn warning.

Lord of All Creation

*And so the Lord Jesus, when he had finished speaking to
them, was taken up to heaven, and is seated now at the
right hand of God.* (Mark 16:19; Gospel of Ascension Day)

The ascension is the triumphant exaltation of Christ.

Jesus of Nazareth, the enfleshed, only-begotten Son of
God, was king by every right from the first moment of His
incarnation. Consider the imperial freedom of His earliest
recorded words, the effortless omnipotence of His initial
miracle, the majestic yet simple character of His every
word and deed. "You are right, I am a king," He answered
quietly to Pilate's mocking charge. Yet this kingship, like
all the attributes of Christ in His mortality, was subject
to and limited by His human condition. Ordinary men
peered at Christ and saw *the carpenter's son.* Antagonists
glared at Christ and saw *this deceiver.* The Roman governor examined Christ and saw *the man.* Flogged and
derisively crowned with thorns, Christ the condemned
criminal made a sad caricature of royalty.

Now, in His ascension, the Lord Christ enters into the
fullness of His kingship. The ascension is the coronation
of King Jesus. He is victorious, He is supreme, He is
unconquerable forever.

But the ascension is even more than our Saviour's personal triumph. Writes Fr. Jean Daniélou: "It is not only visibly above the heavens, it is invisibly above every creature, that Christ's manhood is exalted, amid the awestruck hosts of angelic worlds. . . . This is what makes the ascension the supreme cosmic mystery. Not only does the glorified Christ become the Head of the Church which is His body, but He becomes the Lord of all creation." Immediately one recalls St. Paul's soaring hymn: *God has raised him to such a height, given him that name which is greater than any other name; so that everything in heaven and on earth and under the earth must bend the knee before the name of Jesus, and every tongue must confess Jesus Christ as the Lord, dwelling in the glory of God the Father.*

Perhaps the chief point to grasp about Christ's lordship over all creation is that the Saviour—and the title is here particularly suggestive—does not stand over *against* creation. Christ is the head of all existent reality; He is not its enemy.

Religious thinkers are now in a position to see that the authentic Christian tradition of the dualism, the antithesis, yes, and the antagonism between natural and supernatural, between sacred and profane, between here and hereafter, did become exaggerated. Christians came gradually to suppose that just as (according to their highest authority) they had to choose between God and mammon, so they had to throw in their lot either with Christ or with this present and entrancing world; but not possibly with both. It was this divorce of "faith in God" from "faith in the world" that Teilhard de Chardin saw as the damaging misconception of modern Christianity. Teilhard's keen and healing conviction was that one could know Christ and know the world, love Christ and love the world, serve Christ and serve the world. Reality belongs to the exalted Christ, the sovereign Lord of all creation. He loves it; and so should we.

We quote Fr. Daniélou once more: "The ascension marks the completion of the movement begun at the incarnation, the climax of the action of the divine *agape* in seeking for man to lead him into the realm of the Trinity." But not only man. Somehow, all creation, too.

The Gospel of Triumph

When the truth-giving Spirit, who proceeds from the Father, has come to befriend you, he whom I will send to you from the Father's side, he will bear witness of what I was; and you too are to be my witnesses, you who from the first have been in my company. (John 15:26–27; Gospel of the Sunday after Ascension)

There will be appropriateness in concluding our Paschal season reflections on the Gospel of St. John by attending to the distinctly triumphant tone and quality of that final evangelical witness to the Lord Christ.

The issue here raised is not altogether easy to expound, for we are dealing with one of the subleties of an exceed-

ingly subtle composition; we are noting a cumulative and
atmospheric effect rather than an explicitation. All four
Gospels are triumphant documents in the sense that they
all end with the resurrection of Christ. The difference in
John—the result of what is said, the way in which it is
said, and of what is not said—is that the note of unequivocal, certain, victorious achievement is heard throughout
the Gospel.

As in the Synoptics, the Christ of St. John is portrayed
as steadily involved in conflict; yet there are differences in
the way of unrelenting controversy is recorded. In John
we hear nothing of that which recurs in the Synoptics, the
dialectical trap set by the enemies of the Saviour. (The
first 11 verses of John 8 are in interpolation.) In the
heated exchanges of the fourth Gospel it is always Christ
who takes and holds the initiative. Morover, John admits
no physical assault on our Lord such as that recorded in
Luke 4. True, there are threats of stoning in John, but the
threats quickly come to nothing. *And now they were ready
to seize him; but none of them laid hands on him; his
time had not yet come.* The temple police are dispatched
to arrest Christ. They return empty-handed, muttering un-
easily: *Nobody has ever spoken as this man speaks.*

Again, we find in John nothing corresponding to the
detailed predictions of His passion that our Lord makes in
the Synoptics. On the contrary, the Christ of the last
Gospel speaks repeatedly of what He first terms His *hour*,
and later, *this hour of trial.* But when the time of suffering
comes, the Lord speaks of it as a glory. The wretched
Judas leaves the supper room to complete his treachery.
When he had gone out, Jesus said: Now the Son of Man

has achieved his glory, and in his glory God is exalted.
Then John introduces our Lord's sublime sacerdotal
prayer with these words: *Thus Jesus spoke to them, and
then, lifting up his eyes to heaven, he said: Father, the
time has come; give glory now to your Son, that your Son
may give glory to you.* Three times in John our Lord
speaks of His future death as a being *lifted up,* and the
event is a supreme achievement.

John does not record our Saviour's agony in the garden.
In place of that surprising omission (John, remember, was
one of the three eye-witnesses of the agony), the fourth
Evangelist gives us the curious incident of the demoraliza-
tion of the arresting party as the Lord approaches them.
John also records detailed conversations between Christ
and Pilate, and the whole impression created is that Pilate,
rather than Jesus, stands in deep trouble. According to
John, our Saviour's last word was: *It is achieved.* And
when John (and only John) tells us of the piercing of the
side of Christ upon the cross, the Evangelist is clearly
celebrating what was in every way a triumph.

John Barzebedee is well acquainted with a Christ who
is resented, contradicted, rejected, denied, tortured, put
to death. But John knows nothing of a defeated Christ,
of a Lord and Master who was ever, for a moment, anything less. From first to last, John's soaring hymn to Jesus
is "Hail to the Victor!"

Pentecost and Peace

He who is to befriend you, the Holy Spirit, whom the Father will send on my account, will in his turn make everything plain, and recall to your minds everything I have said to you. Peace is my bequest to you, and the peace which I give is mine to give. (John 14:26–27; Gospel of Pentecost)

The juxtaposition of these two verses in the Gospel of St. John may be noticed. Our Lord, speaking to His disciples in the serene intimacy of the Last Supper, makes a promise. *The Holy Spirit . . . will in his turn make everything plain, and recall to your minds everything I have said to you.* The Lord then leaves a legacy: *Peace is my bequest to you.* We may conclude, then, that the Holy Spirit, when he comes upon the followers of Christ, will clarify, deepen and reinforce the *peace* that the Saviour has bestowed. St. Paul says as much: *The kingdom of God . . . means rightness of heart, finding our peace and our joy in the Holy Spirit. Such is the badge of Christ's service.*

In the conviction of a continuing, ever new coming of the Holy Spirit upon men of faith, we Christians gladly keep the present festival of Pentecost. It may be, though, that we find ourselves recalling, however unwillingly, the prophetic lament of Jeremias: *Peace, peace—and there is no peace.*

According to the classic definition of St. Augustine, peace is the "tranquillity of order." Amid the clashing and agitation of the contemporary religious world, the Christian man looks longingly about him and within him for some degree of tranquillity, and may even wonder whether anything like order survives in the dimension of faith. When the human mind is able to repose in established certainties and the individual conscience is sincerely aware of essential rectitude, interior peace will ensue. When, in the external forum of religion, solid consensus exists over a wide area of belief, and controversy is both peripheral and restrained, there will then be an open and experienced "tranquillity of order." Suppose, however, that religious controversy rages over the most fundamental questions both of belief and of morals. Will anyone then be surprised if Pentecostal peace appears to exist only as a fond recollection?

It might be profitable if, at this newest Pentecost, we were to read again and with new attention the New Testament book that immediately follows the four Gospels. There we will not only read of the original descent of the Holy Spirit upon the nascent Church, but come to realize, it may be with some surprise, that the flaming Spirit of God did *not* bring to the original Christian family what we would comfortably regard as peace. The coming of the Paraclete led directly to persecution of the little Christian band. The coming of the Spirit was soon followed by internal disturbances (Ananias and Sapphira), unholy tendencies (the first appearance of simony), and controversy so prolonged and so divisive that a Council had to be called for the sake of some tranquility of order.

Peace is an ideal that will always and naturally and powerfully attract the human heart. Yet we must acknowledge that peace as an absolute ideal can be illusory, and the pursuit of it can end in escapism. The stillness that is taken as a sure sign of peace can be the stillness of timidity, it can be the complete stillness of death. A certain recorded statement of Christ might be recalled in connection with our observance of the newest Pentecost: *Do not think that I have come to bring peace on earth. I have not come to bring peace, but a sword.*

Come, Holy Spirit, we rightly pray. His coming may not always be exactly what we had in mind.

Mystery and Majesty

How deep is the mine of God's wisdom, of his knowledge; how inscrutable are his judgments, how undiscoverable his ways! Who has ever understood the Lord's thoughts, or been his counselor? (Romans 11:33–34; Epistle of Trinity Sunday)

There could hardly be a more apt occasion than Trinity Sunday on which to note, once more and not for the last time, the important distinction between what men religiously believe and the way in which they will express what they believe.

The whole immense problem that we now designate as the issue of semantics is not exactly a recent discovery. It has always been recognized that the tools we call *words* are not only marvelously useful (and often beautiful) but also distressingly unreliable. The poet who protested: "One word is too often profaned/For me to profant it" never, presumably, had heard of semantics, but he was aware of the problem. Besides, the basic reason why writers steadily feel sorry for themselves is that they constantly experience the desolating anguish of trying to express in words *exactly* what is churning and burning inside themselves.

So, then: if language is a tricky tool at best, and if men find it endlessly difficult to describe precisely what is going on inside them, can anyone be surprised if man encounters very special trouble in describing what goes on (if we may so speak without irreverance) inside God?

No doubt there is gain in the fact that God is currently news. The drawback is the consequent tendency to treat the good news of the Christian God like any other news. Every reporter knows that his job is to get the facts of the story with absolute accuracy. Every rewrite man knows that his job is to assemble the data in a story that will be smooth and lean and utterly clear. Every editor knows that the story must be presented in the place and context where it will have maximum impact. Good, good. Now what are we to do with the story of God? How are we to expose, in quickly comprehensible terms, the mystery and majesty of God? How are we to follow up, in cool, lucid prose, a lead like this? *How deep is the mine of God's wisdom, of his knowledge; how inscrutable are his judgments, how undiscoverable his ways! Who has ever understood the Lord's thoughts, or been his counselor?*

Complaint could be made that in the passage quoted St. Paul may be praying, may even be waxing lyrical, but is not really answering any questions. The complaint is groundless. Paul is answering our questions about God by pointing to the mystery and majesty of God.

There is danger that much of the present talk about God could actually cheapen our concept of God. One senses some sort of suggestion that God is being called upon to stand and deliver; to prove Himself; to make Himself clear, really clear, once and for all. One catches a hint of deep-down vulgarity in the search for a neatly packaged Deity who will stand up under journalistic and television examination. If God behaves Himself and meets our minimal demands, we will grant Him a proper place in our reasonable, jolly, bomb-haunted, anthropocentric universe. Otherwise, let Him look to be picketed, and then ignored.

God is one; Father, Son and Holy Spirit are three. Is this compound proposition comprehensible? No. We who are Christians believe it; we accept it in faith. We welcome the mystery of God, which does not surprise us, and we adore the majesty of God, which impresses and consoles us.

Times Change

My flesh is real food, my blood is real drink. He who eats my flesh, and drinks my blood, lives continually in me, and I in him. (John 6:56–57; Gospel for the Feast of Corpus Christi)

Words are signs. Inevitably, then, words are signs of the times. In the vocabulary of religion, as elsewhere, it is always instructive to observe the rise and fall of particular expressions. A generation ago, Catholics always spoke of "hearing" Mass, and the old Irish used to request the priest to "read" a Mass for their intention. The present venerable writer has no recollection of encountering, in his green and callow youth, such terms as "salvation history" and "personalism" and "ecumenism"—though he minds well numerous references to a mysterious "A.P.A.," references that definitely lacked ecumenical flavor. "Dialogue," of course, was something that took place in a play, and "hell," in addition to serving as a useful expletive, was the reasonable, pyrotechnic destiny of all who crudely ate meat on Fridays or rudely spoke ill of the Pope.

Tempora mutantur: Times change. (The quotation is in Latin, a language once widely employed in the Catholic Church.) Among religious terms that have lost or are losing the patina of respectability, we must include the word "devotion"—especially when it is used in the plural.

That a multiplicity of peripheral devotions has exercised a generally negative effect on Catholic spirituality
is a view that can hardly be challegened. In fairness,
though, we must attend to certain words here, too: "multiplicity" and "peripheral."

When, in any human situation or enterprise, more and
more practical attention is given to what is more and
more distant from the heart of the matter, the inevitable
result must be, at the least, waste, and, more likely, grave
distortion of the reality involved. Catholicism has suffered
from too many and too local saints, too many alleged
"revelations," too many dubious miracles, too much regard for supposed relics, too much concern for the mathe-
matics of indulgences, too many vigil candles before too
many atrocious statues. Add: too many holy cards with
verses that, to coin a phrase, would make the angels weep.

All the more reason, then, why we should magnify and
assiduously cultivate those devotions, those modes or
forms of true piety, that rest on the most solid theological
foundations, that involve the deepest truths of our religion, that are, therefore, central in Catholic life and
faith and practice.

Such a cultus is devotion to the Eucharist. That which
is honored here is not a thing or a place or a memory, but
a Person. That Person is Christ. Christ is honored in the
recollection of His deeds and destiny; He is adored in His
now present, living reality as Lord.

That reality comes about through the supreme and
perfect act of worship, the Mass. Singular union with the
living, present Christ results from the simple act of eating;

for the sign of the Lord's actual presence is bread and wine.

My flesh is real food, my blood is real drink. He who eats my flesh, and drinks my blood, lives continually in me, and I in him. In this holy supper, the earnest convivialists are bound anew not only to Christ but to one another. Finally, all who eat receive another pledge and promise of eternal contentment.

Devotion in the Church wants looking after, and devotions would benefit by curtailment. But the festival of Corpus Christi will not fall from our liturgical calendar any more than the Eucharist could vanish from our altars and our tabernacles.

The Sign Still Signifies

There was a man that gave a great supper, and sent out many invitations. And when the time came for his supper, he sent one of his own servants telling the invited guests to come, for all was now ready. (Luke 14:16–17; Gospel of the Second Sunday after Pentecost)

The *great supper,* the festive, social, all-satisfying banquet, was repeatedly used by the Lord Christ in His teaching as an image of that *kingdom of heaven* whose present advent the Saviour was proclaiming. As Christians listen again to the parable of *a great supper,* but hear it now on the Sunday nearest the feast of Corpus Christi, they will naturally be reminded of the mystery of the Eucharist. Then, perhaps, Christian men and women of the present religious perplexity may wonder whether the Church's understanding of the Eucharistic mystery is less tidy, much more blurry in outline, than it once was. Despite the forbidding technical term, the majority of Catholics have probably entertained a tolerably clear notion of what was essentially meant by *transubstantiation.* But what in the blue-eyed Christian world is *transignification?* It is evident to all of us that we still have the Eucharist. *What* do we have in the Eucharist?

Vatican II replied, and in the most traditional language, to this question. In the Eucharist we have been given a presence, a food, a bond and a promise.

In all discussion of the Christian religion, which not only countenances but embraces and proclaims mystery, attention must ever be called to the permanent distinction between a religious truth and the available explanation of that truth. Perhaps, in answer to the question *"How* is Christ actually present in the Eucharist?", it would be best to reply: "We do not know." What matters is not the explanation but the fact. The fact is that the living Christ is actually present in the Eucharist. On this day and in the present hour, the earnest follower of Christ ought to let his mind fix firmly and immovably and happily on that fact.

The Eucharist is food, and food is nourishment, and the spiritual life of man must, like his physical life, be nourished. Here the Christian must steady his mind with

a pair of uncomplicated considerations. First, there is the
real difference (acknowledged, in degree, even in physical
life) between being nourished, therefore growing stronger,
and feeling nourished or feeling stronger. Grace is simply
not experienced on the level of sensation. Feeling, warm
or otherwise, has nothing significant to do with the recep-
tion of the Eucharist. Second, the contemporary Christian
must resolutely and reasonably refuse to allow the rude (?)
clamor of high (?) theological warfare to mar the peace and
upset the peaceful procedure of his own sacramental life.

The Eucharist, declared Vatican II, is "a sacrament of
love, a sign of unity, a bond of charity." As is well understood, that love, that unity, that charity, is both vertical
(between God and man) and horizontal (between man and
man). Without the vertical, the horizontal is not religion
but humanism. Without the horizontal, the vertical is not
religion—certainly not the Christian religion—but pious
flummery.

"And a pledge of future glory is given to us." Thus the
Council concludes its first full statement on the Eucharist.
It is deplorable, of course, that the Council Fathers not
only employed such classic language in connection with
the Eucharist, but ignored the sensibilities of all the hyper-
activated neo-Christians who are increasingly distressed by
reference to any existence but the present one. To some
of us, though, that "future glory" looks better and better
with every passing—note: *passing*—moment.

Without Sentimentality

But when they came to Jesus, and found him already dead, they did not break his legs, but one of the soldiers opened his side with a spear; and immediately blood and water flowed out. (John 19:33–34; Gospel for the Feast of the Sacred Heart)

In the updating, the modernization, of the Catholic Church—at a time when "devotions" are being re-examined in terms of Scripture and authentic tradition, when, so to speak, piety is dieting so as to shed the excess fat of centuries—what are we to think and say of devotion to the Sacred Heart? Is it in any way central to the Christian thing, or is it peripheral and therefore expendable?

Let it be conceded at once that the problem here is not nearly as simple as is the question of the Eucharist.

Three objections could be brought against devotion to the Sacred Heart. First, the formal, explicit cultus is of comparatively recent origin. We cannot summon the apostolic or post-apostolic Church as witness to this devotion, for it is not yet 300 years old. Next, the explicit honoring of the Heart of Christ began with a private revelation (a divine communication to an individual, as distinct from God's public revelation of truth to and through the teaching Church), and private revelation has ever constituted a thorny problem in Christian history. Third, Sacred Heart devotion has been taxed with that which can be ruinous in religion as elsewhere—excessive sentimentality.

Perhaps the most honest answer to make to these strictures is that they are true. Yet difficulties, even when real, must be carefully weighed.

We hear much today of the development of doctrine in the Church. Now, it would be curious if, under the guidance of the Spirit, we were to glimpse new facets of revealed truth and yet experience no parallel advance in religious practice; if, that is, there could be no practical implementation of a fresh intuition into our faith. What is demanded of any devotional departure in the Church is that it be strictly in accord with revealed truth. Surely, we may assert without partisanship that the theological foundations of the Sacred Heart cultus have been firmly established. What we have here is devotion to Christ the Incarnate Word in His state as victim.

It is always helpful to recall what is and what is not involved when the teaching, authoritative Church "approves" a private revelation. The Church's endorsement extends *only* to the strict theological content of the communication, and no judgment is passed on the historical circumstances or content in which attention is now drawn to some particular aspect of religious truth already essentially known. What matters in this devotion is not Margaret Mary and her words, but Christ and His love. The truth of Christ as victim and the idea of atonement or reparation for sin are by no means 300 years young.

Sentimentality always threatens to intrude whenever we start to talk about Mom and precious babies and our country, right or wrong, and man's best friend, the noble dog. Indeed, the heart is a symbol that has taken unusual punishment in this regard. Yet it must be remembered that a symbol, even when it has been long abused, still symbolizes—especially on the most popular level. Devotion to the Sacred Heart has made Christ and His love most vividly and convincingly real to many an earnest, uncomplicated follower of Christ.

Let us without sentimentality, and certainly without embarrassment, welcome the feast of the Sacred Heart.

The Perennial Piety

When they found all the publicans and sinners coming to listen to him, the Pharisees and scribes were indignant; Here is a man, they said, that entertains sinners, and eats with them. (Luke 15:1–2; Gospel of the Third Sunday after Pentecost)

In the living worship of the Church, "devotions" wax and wane. The fact need disturb no one; piety, always influenced by psychology, will take successive forms. In certain connections, however, the question of changing piety becomes significant. Will Marian devotion change? If so, how? Will there be alteration in devotion to the Eucharist?

Why or why not? Is there place in the renewed Church for devotion to the Sacred Heart? Does this cultus, with its sentiment and simplicity, more properly belong to what may now be recognized as the adolescent time in the long life of the Church?

It becomes increasingly necessary to call attention to the essential, as distinct from the picturesque, elements in devotion to the Heart of Christ.

The designation, "Heart of Christ," accurately points out the first essential factor in this cultus. What is honored in devotion to the Sacred Heart is the Person, Jesus of Nazareth, the Incarnate Word of God. Obvious as it may seem, the point must be emphasized. The question here is that of honor paid not to a favored or local or possibly non-existent saint, nor even of that special regard which Catholics fondly tender to Mary ever Virgin. Devotion to the Sacred Heart is honor paid to Christ Jesus. It involves the profound considerations of Christology and soteriology. It raises the question of the personal relationship between the Christian and Christ. Even at first glance, therefore, this cultus will scarcely be regarded as a passing or fanciful form of Christian worship. You may, so to speak, take an individual saint or leave him. By definition, the Christian has and wants no such option with reference to Christ.

Objection has at times been made that the imagery and language of devotion to the Sacred Heart are not free from a strong flavor of sentimentality. The objection must be allowed. There is place here, however, for renewed attention to the distinction between a truth and the mode in which that truth is expressed. The primary stress, the pre-

cise point, in devotion to the Heart of Christ is love. No
doubt the point is sometimes made in terms that cheapen
the actuality. But one might expect that the actuality
would yet appeal with special force to a generation of
Catholics with whom the veritable love-over-law thesis has
become a passion. The heart as a symbol may now be a
tired symbol, but what is symbolized has never been
more religiously or sociologically in favor. It is exactly
that—personal, experienced love—which is the essence of
devotion to the Sacred Heart.

Yet another factor in this cultus is or ought to be part
of the permanent essence of religion. It is a sense of sin.

It may be freely admitted that a certain amount of moral
teaching in religion has not been psychologically sound;
popular preaching has always tended to bear down heavily
on the case against sin. If the human being (and particularly the child) is made to feel guilty of wrong when in fact
he is not guilty of wrong, that person is diminished and
damaged. If anyone, having done wrong, is led to feel
disproportionately or frantically guilty, again that person
is diminished and damaged. After this element of excess
in traditional religious exhortation has been conceded,
there remains such a thing as conscious moral evil; and
one who freely does conscious moral evil *ought* to feel
guilty. In short, religion, without lapsing into pessimism,
ought to retain a sense of sin. There is no need for invention or morbid fantasy. In this matter, the actuality will
serve.

A sense of sin is prominent in devotion to the Sacred
Heart. What is to be noted is that sin is here seen as a
failure in personal love; that the lapse is deplored, and

loving atonement made for it; that the emphasis is not on the degree of guilt, but on the slight to love.

The feast of the Sacred Heart is to be celebrated with joy and affection; not with embarrassment.

Fishers of Men

But Jesus said to Simon, Do not be afraid; henceforth thou shalt be a fisher of men. So, when they had brought their boats to land, they left all and followed him. (Luke 5:10–11; Gospel of the Fourth Sunday after Pentecost)

It is clearly important that we make an earnest effort—one can only try—to understand the existing vocational situation which presently may become a full-blown crisis.

First, some rectification must be attempted of the spreading suspicion that priests and religious are, by and large, an unhappy and fairly useless lot. We will readily concede that somehow the Church, an institution with a markedly human side, has not employed and deployed its manpower with anything like maximum efficiency. Still, one might engage in a highly instructive fantasy by imagining himself rising some fair morning to a Catholic world in which (to use a single but significant example) there were no nuns. It would be a necessitous world; appallingly so. That morning would not be fair at all.

As for the question of contentment and fulfillment among priests and religious, it really should be urged that the spate of publicized and garrulous and abusive departures from consecrated life has created an impression that is simply and flatly false. The overwhelming majority of religiously dedicated men and women continue stanchly to believe not only in the living and loving God they have always known (the One that isn't dead or even ailing), but in the reliability of revealed truth, the divine element in the Church, the strict necessity of humble prayer, the value of their calling, and—we add firmly—celibacy. Even while they wonder and maybe worry about many grave problems, people equipped with such a set of convictions are apt to be radically contented.

As has been widely remarked, the decline in vocations must be understood as pointing the way to the new status and function of the layman in the Catholic Church. The priest and religious of tomorrow will do priestly and religious work; the rest—not because it is second-rate work, but because it is now so clearly his job—will be done by the apostolic layman. There are so many tasks that must daily be discharged in the ample household of the Church, tasks that are administrative, financial, educational, promotional, technical, *secular,* that strictly do not pertain to the priest or religious in his truest reality and that the skilled layman may be expected to perform with superior results. Of course, such a structure in the working Church is going to cost money; and here is a growing problem that the Church, and especially the layman in the Church, will be called upon to deal with.

As this day's Gospel vividly reminds us of the reality of

priestly and religious vocation, we may justly entertain the consoling expectation that the young men and young women who will now heed the personal invitation of Christ to them will compensate qualitatively for whatever will soon be lacking quantitatively. With all its pains, the evident and needed renewal of priesthood and religious life in the Church will increasingly offer to the most likely young people solid promise of a life that is indeed worth living: a life of both dedication and fulfillment, of high obligation and authentic freedom, of total sacrifice and total reward.

Christian Controversy

And I tell you that if your justice does not give fuller measure than the justice of the scribes and Pharisees, you shall not enter into the kingdom of heaven. (Matthew 5:20; Gospel of the Fifth Sunday after Pentecost)

It is not at all necessary to read this particular exhortation of the Lord Christ as an attack upon the moral code of His day. The Saviour is simply saying that His religious system will set up for its adherents loftier moral standards than men have hitherto acknowledged.

After the general admonition, our Lord turns to the specific problem of hostility between men. There seems no special reason why people 2,000 years ago should have been more antagonistic to one another than people are now. Men are men, and the reasons why they quarrel differ only on the surface. For one thing, men have always entertained differing views of questions that concern them, and they have always argued for their views. Well and good; for a variety of reasons, controversy is beneficial. On the basis of the Saviour's directives that we hear today, we may conclude that there is a Christian manner of engaging in controversy.

Everyone understands why religious controversy in the Catholic Church is presently raging. The explanation is simple: the dam has burst. Would it here be out of place to enter into some small, low-key controversy on the subject of Christian controversy?

People should have convictions—which is merely another way of saying that people should be genuinely alive, and not half asleep, moribund or interiorly missing from the scene. Next, people ought to express those convictions, most especially when the matter at issue is weighty with serious consequences. There remains the question, both socially and religiously important, of *how* convictions should be expressed, of how controversy ought to be conducted by civilized men of religious belief.

Such men should argue with modesty and moderation; with conspicuous absence of malice and mockery.

We will not allow that such a wonderfully alliterative prescription must reduce all controversy to gentle, anesthetic murmurings that are predestined to issue in nothing but a drowsy euphoria. Argument should be sharp, debate ought to be keen, controversy must be wholehearted. We only urge that certain rational and familiar principles of argumentation—such as the distinction between the issue and the persons at issue—be kept somewhere available in the arguing mind.

It should be stressed, for example, that controversy is an enterprise of the intellect, not of the emotions. Admittedly, when a person becomes totally involved in a question, the total person will be involved. Nevertheless, the Christian in controversy ought to be and remain that. He should have a mind to modesty and moderation; he must forego the scarcely veiled malice of the *man who is angry with his brother;* he has no title to the cruel, calculating, clever mockery that says, save for the word, *You fool.*

Now we might profitably reread, and seriously ponder, the final sentence in this day's second liturgical reading.

The Church of the Poor

Once more, at this time, the multitude had grown in numbers, and had nothing to eat. And he called his disciples to him, and said to them, I am moved with pity for the multitude . . . they have nothing to eat. (Mark 8:1–2; Gospel of the Sixth Sunday after Pentecost)

The exceedingly complex problem of the Church and poverty has two main aspects: how poverty is to be served by the Church, and how poverty is to be observed in the Church.

There can be no doubt that a state of actual poverty is held up as a religious ideal in the teaching of the four Gospels. Our Lord's directive to a prospective close follower—*Sell all that belongs to you, and give it to the poor; so the treasure you have shall be in heaven; then come back and follow me*—is recorded in almost identical terms by all three Synoptics; and we perceive that the directive includes both concern for the poor and concern to be poor. Our Saviour is quoted as expressing, more than once, notably severe views on the relationship between wealth and what we regard as salvation. His most celebrated hyperbole was employed in this connection. *With what difficulty will those who have riches enter God's kingdom! It is easier for a camel to pass through a needle's eye, than for a man to enter the kingdom of God when he is rich.* The heavy villain in one of the Saviour's short stories is traditionally known as Dives, but in the parable he has no name. Dives is the Latin word for *rich man*.

Yet the Gospel picture is actually not as clear as all that. Our Lord and His followers unquestionably accepted gifts of money, and Christ explicitly affirmed the right of the apostolic laborer to support and recompense. There was an apostolic purse or treasury that was the responsibility of Judas Iscariot—why not Matthew? Curious—a purse that allowed some degree of almsgiving. Somehow the impression is created that the Saviour's intimate friends in Bethany, the Lazarus-Martha-Mary family, were comfortably well-off, and certainly the hero of our Lord's burial was wealthy Joseph of Arimathea.

The Church's history in the matter of wealth and poverty has been strongly marked by the ambivalence that

appears in the Gospels. The Church has sung the praises
of voluntary poverty as a religious value, and beyond dis-
pute has in countless ways and enterprises sought to relieve
the needs of the poor. Yet the institutional Church has
accumulated assets (as well as debts), the Church has
courted people of wealth, priests, and religious generally
live in comfort and sometimes in affluence. Moreover, the
presence of the Church has not been especially notable in
the urban ghettos where the really poor of our time swarm
and swelter and very nearly starve.

It is easy to complain bitterly of what may be regarded
as either the Church's lack of realism or its quite cynical
realism on the issue of wealth and poverty. Whether such
complaint would itself be entirely realistic, just and balanced is another question. But the hour is too late for
blame and the distribution of blame. What matters is that
the Church is slowly and surely coming to the realization
that, in this critical area of have and have-not, the household of the faith must be set in order. The Church turns
more and more concernedly to the inner city and its teem-
ing, hapless multitudes. Sincere priests and religious grow
more acutely uncomfortable in their comfort. More and
more painful questions are being asked. What does it
mean to undertake to live the life of a poor man? What
must we *do* to prove that the Christian Church truly re-
tains the mind and heart of Christ, who said, *I am moved
with pity for the multitude . . . they have nothing to eat.*

The Christian millennium may be as far away as ever.
On the other hand, there are one or two signs that all is
not lost.

False Prophets?

Be on your guard against false prophets, men who come to you in sheep's clothing, but are ravenous wolves within. You will know them by the fruit they yield. (Matthew 7:15–16; Gospel of the Seventh Sunday after Pentecost)

The New Testament writers are much concerned about the danger that arises for the Christian revelation from the teaching of *false prophets*. Matthew puts upon the lips of Christ three warnings on the subject, one of which is repeated by Mark. St. Paul is in a constant fret because of *false apostles, false brethren*. Both Peter and John, in their letters, speak of *false prophets,* and the Apocalypse three times mentions *the false prophet,* who is associated with those monstrous forces of evil called *the beast* and *the dragon*. Such worry on the part of the earliest Christian writers is understandable. The maximum peril for nascent Christianity was that it should be corrupted doctrinally at the very outset.

In the Sermon on the Mount, our Saviour both excoriates *false prophets*—they are *men who come to you in sheep's clothing, but are ravenous wolves within*—but also provides the touchstone by which they can be identified. *You will know them by the fruit they yield.*

The Saviour of the world, whom St. Paul justly calls

Christ the power of God, Christ the wisdom of God, will know that we intend no petulant complaint when we suggest that His sharp discussion of *false prophets* leaves us of this present time with something of a double problem.

In what seems an era, disturbed and disturbing, of unprecedented intramural religious controversy, how shall we followers of Christ learn to distinguish teachers of error from teachers of truth? *You will know them by the fruit they yield.* The principle cannot be faulted. In the long run, error will issue in evil of one kind or another, truth will be fruitful of good. The difficulty lies in the necessary and considerable time-lapse between seeding and harvest. How can religious and especially Christian man identify the false prophet *now?* And if the propagandist of religious error cannot be known *now,* how does the man of sincere religious faith conduct himself until the advent of what journalists uncontrollably call "the moment of truth"?

The second difficulty is yet more troublesome. Even in the extreme religious differences of our day, there is no indication that the moral and doctrinal teachers *who come to us in sheep's clothing* are anything but what they seem to be: honest—if endlessly articulate and irrepressible— sheep with unimpeachable sheepskins. Whatever we may think of the various religious views that are currently ventilated, we cannot doubt that the spokesmen intend and hope to put in a saving word for God, the Church, the truth and a decent human future. The religious clamor may be deafening, but it is not dishonest, not malicious. The manifest and even humorless earnestness of the combatants is the problem. Not often in its exciting history,

has Christianity witnessed such diversity of religous insights coupled with such sincere conviction that so many
insights are wrong.

Our Lord's instruction of this day may be understood as
reminding us who believe in Him of a couple of truths
that we must keep in view. For example, that we live in a
religiously chancy time. We know it; yet we will be advised, and walk carefully in our pilgrim way. Christ suggests also that we be patient in our pursuit of the good
and the true. One of our Saviour's agricultural similarities
warns against tearing up an entire crop because we don't
like the early look of it.

Be on your guard. Noted, Lord. But please keep us from
false alarms as well as from *false prophets.*

Evolution in Christian Values

*Brethren, nature has no longer any claim on us, that we
should live a life of nature. If you live a life of nature,
you are marked out for death; if you mortify the ways of
nature through the power of the Spirit, you will have life.*
(Romans 8:12–13; Epistle of the Eighth Sunday after
Pentecost)

Let it be granted that the term *nature,* which appears four
times in our brief text, is not only a familiar word, but a

difficult one; a word that slips through the mental grasp like water through the fingers; a word more elusive than *spirit*. Setting aside, then, all precisions, we are led by St. Paul's remarks of this day to consider anew the classical Christian distinction between natural and supernatural.

Convenient distinctions—those that appear immediately clear and immediately applicable—always tend in use to become unduly enlarged. One thinks straightway of the distinction between the man whose skin happens to be black and the man whose skin happens to be white. It is not surprising that popular Christian exposition gradually so separated supernatural from natural that the two became not only strangers but enemies. Natural values were denigrated, natural motives were suspect, natural impulses were naturally stained in their source; is not original sin a self-evident reality? What mattered, almost exclusively, was the supernatural: God and God's service, godly virtue, strictly religious values, the "pure intention." The conclusion of the quite sincere argument was obvious. This world of time, with all its issues, works and pomps (*there's a fine word!*), is inconsequential, not worth bothering about. The only point of time is eternity.

No doubt there has been more than one total reaction to a trend or mood in the long history of Christianity, but one may question whether there has ever been a more hearty assault on a previous value-judgment than the present religious rejection of the hopeless estrangement between natural and supernatural. Man, man as he is here and now, man in and with the "nature" that God gave him, man in his present hungers and crying needs, man in his psychology and sociology, man with his fearful

dilemma of war and peace—that man is what matters, not
only to himself, but to his institutional religion. It will no
longer serve, indeed it is not honest or of God, that man
should ask for bread and the Church should soothingly
offer him the stone, however precious, of eternal reple-
tion. There is profound religious as well as sociological
significance in the current rallying cry of the man whose
skin is black. He demands freedom, and whatever else is
due him, *now*.

The Christian reaction in favor of temporal values, of
man in the here and now, represents an authentic evolution (it often looks sufficiently like a reversal) of Christian
values. No one will allege that in the past Christianity was
ever the implacable enemy of immediate human concerns,
for the story of Christian art, science and charity gives the
lie to such a charge. Still, there was the strong bias in the
favor of the unseen, the immaterial, the eternal. Christianity, you see, was and is a religion. It has something to do
with God and eternity as well as with man and time.

We will honestly rejoice that the challenge of authentic
prophets like Teilhard de Chardin to the natural-super-
natural dichotomy has been sustained by the contemporary
Church. We will recognize that men, with all their unfailing concerns, are likely to be here on earth for a very long
time to come. We will also consider thoughtfully that *we*
men won't be here.

The Helplessness of Christ

And as he drew near, and caught sight of the city, he wept over it, and said: Ah, if you too could understand, above all in this day that is granted you, the ways that can bring you peace! As it is, they are hidden from your sight. (Luke 19:41; Gospel of the Ninth Sunday after Pentecost)

It was the morning of the first Palm Sunday. As the joyful parade in honor of Jesus the Prophet rounded a turn in the Bethany road, the Holy City, white and brilliant in the golden sunlight, burst into view. The Saviour's excited companions cheered more lustily than ever, the pace of the procession quickened as it marched toward some unclear but certain triumph, every face was flushed with gladness. And tears ran down the face of Christ. There before Him sparkled the beloved city. Sharply etched in His prophetic mind's eye was the horrid image of Sion scorched and silent, razed and desolate. Christ wept.

The believer in Christ feels a sudden pang of distress. Here was a crisis. Here was an impending catastrophe, with so much of human weal and woe at stake. Here, fully involved, is the wise, loving, powerful Redeemer of mankind. Is He helpless before the horror that threatens? In this fearful situation, can He do nothing but weep?

Correct. Looking out over the doomed Jerusalem, the

Lord of heaven and earth can do nothing but weep. He had already done all He could. *Jerusalem, Jerusalem . . . how often have I been ready to gather your children together, as a hen gathers her chickens under her wings; and you refused it!* His mighty power extends serenely over the forces of nature, over disease and physical blindness and even bodily death, over the devils themselves; but not, by way of force, over the heart of man. Christ, *the true likeness of the God we cannot see,* does not violate the free will of man. This Lord will rule by love, or not at all. It is frightening to realize that upon occasion, after the divine love has been offered and offered again and offered yet again, the final word of Christ must be: *You refused it.*

For all we know, the world of time, and therefore the Church in time, may yet be in infancy or adolescence. All dire warnings about the imminence of the last trump have thus far proved hasty and ill-advised. Both the world and the Church have yet much to learn from experience; and we may suggest, guardedly, that both, in fact, are learning. The Church, for example, is learning to rule by love and in no other way. More significant than it may have appeared at the time was the formal retraction, by Pope Paul and Patriarch Athenagoras, of the ancient, mutual excommunications. It has been remarked that when furious Simon Peter slashed at the ear of the enemy in Gethsamene, he did exactly what made it impossible for the enemy to listen to him or to anyone else in the foreseeable future.

Further, the helplessness of Christ before the human will is itself a homily for the human heart. If men object to coercion, well and good; but then let them throw themselves fully open to reason, to reflection and especially to love. If Christ will rule only by love, by love we must consent to be ruled.

You refused. The terrible indictment may be more mournful than menacing. For him who reads, as for him who writes, it must not be true.

Confidence and Arrogance

There were some who had confidence in themselves, thinking they had won acceptance with God, and despised the rest of the world; to them he addressed this parable: Two men went up into the temple to pray . . . (Luke 18:9–10; Gospel of the Tenth Sunday after Pentecost)

It is common doctrine among ethicians, moralists and ascetics of whatever competence or stripe that the character trait we term "humility" presents a pretty problem, indeed. Now that we know more than we did about depth psychology, the puzzle has become more intricate than ever. One is reminded of the familiar pronouncement of the *Imitation of Christ:* "I had rather experience contrition than be able to define it"—and finds himself muttering grumpily about monkish escapism.

Most obvious, of course, is the fact that humility has little to do with the habitual manner in which a man speaks about himself. Here is another of those instances in which talk is not only cheap, but misleading. Proud people will verbally belittle themselves, and some genuinely humble men retain through life the absurd boastfulness of the little boy. But humility does involve an interior judgment concerning oneself in relation to others, and then demands behaivor in accordance with it.

Nemo sui judex, runs the old, remembered tag in the old, forgotten language: "No one is a proper judge in his own case." Self-regard, subtle and stubborn, makes truly objective judgment about oneself as difficult as any single operation a human being can undertake. Certain men remain blissfully aware that they have never made a completely objective judgment in the course of their lives, and certain women couldn't care less about objective judgment under any circumstances. None the less, humility requires the most impersonal personal judgment concerning one's own inner person, about that person in relation both to God and to other men.

It's a tricky business. One comes to realize that what appears to be arrogance can be the most selfless if tactless zeal for truth, and that diffidence can cover a towering pride. A reason why individuals refuse to compete is that they cannot bear to lose and especially be seen to lose.

What makes the question of humility particularly relevant at the moment is the wild proliferation of religious controversy. Everyone is now urged (sometimes unnecessarily) to have and express an opinion in matters religious; charisms, like pentecostal confetti, are all over the place. Everyone wants to speak his piece, speak it firmly, speak it now. Speaking one's piece invariably means contradict-

ing the preceding piece-speaker. How may this performance be accomplished with confidence, yet without arrogance? How may and should a Christian speaker voice a
conviction with conviction and not simultaneously imply
that he who holds an opposite conviction with conviction
is a dimwit, a sloth who has shamefully neglected his
homework, a hollow voice from the pre-scientific past, a
figure of fun, a pious Donald Duck parading as Jeremias
redivivus?

What troubles one is not that this issue of Christian
humility—this real problem of real arrogance under the
cloak of confidence—is not solved, but that it is not seen.
So many zealous people seem worried lest they miss the
chance to speak and be heard. Few seem to worry about
how they speak and how they sound when they are heard,
and whether the keen thrust they are making will draw
blood rather than pierce error.

That devout Pharisee was a *very* confident and articulate fellow.

The Finger of God

*And he took him aside out of the multitude; he put his
fingers into his ears, and spat, and touched his tongue;
then he looked up to heaven, and sighed: Ephpheta, he
said (that is, Be opened). Whereupon his ears were opened,*

and the bond which tied his tongue was loosed, and he spoke plainly. (Mark 7:33–35; Gospel of the Eleventh Sunday after Pentecost)

Commenting on this highly detailed Marcan narrative, Pope St. Gregory notices one gesture of Christ in healing the sorely handicapped man: *he put his fingers into his ears.* Gregory is reminded of a remark of the Saviour in connection with a different miracle: *It is through the finger of God that I cast out devils.* But Matthew's version of that saying is: *When I cast out devils, I do it through the Spirit of God.* Gregory's conclusion, that one of the names or images for the Holy Spirit is "the finger of God," is enshrined in the principal liturgical hymn of Pentecost. The image suggests the irresistible, often miraculous power of the Spirit.

Does the contemporary Christian find himself wondering, now and again, why the presence and activity of the Holy Spirit are no longer as startlingly demonstrated as they were in the time of Christ, no longer as unmistakably experienced by believers as they were in the early Church?

"The Christian religion," writes biblical scholar Alan Richardson, "owes its existence to the intensity of the conviction of the apostolic Church that the outpouring of the Spirit had taken place; the Church's experience of the Spirit was proof that the Messianic age had arrived and that the prophecies of the Scriptures were fulfilled in Jesus Christ."

The puzzle, though not necessarily the essential point in the matter, is what Dr. Richardson calls "the Church's experience of the Spirit." This actual, emphatic *experience,* manifested (we will grant) in ways not all of which we now find congenial, was overwhelmingly real. The fact is that we no longer enjoy this strong, personal experience of the Spirit, which played so influential a part in both the missionary activity and the intramural life of the primitive Christian Church.

Before we conclude that the Holy Spirit is neglecting us believers of a later day, let us ask a few questions.

As has been observed on other occasions, it may be that both this world of time and the Church in it are still, according to God's eternal calendar, very young indeed. On the other hand, the Christian family must be considered to have achieved, in some two thousand years, a degree of spiritual maturity. Is the smashing experience of the Spirit as necessary now as it once was?

Suppose that such palpable experience of the Spirit of God, together with its typical manifestations as seen in the New Testament, were to occur now. How would it be received and esteemed? What would depth psychology say of it?

Is it not a fact, recorded by the Holy Spirit, that St. Paul, who never tires of speaking of the power of the Spirit, made every effort to discourage the more spectacular manifestations of the experience of the Spirit?

The true issue is plain. Are there now solid signs or manifestations, but of a different kind, that the Holy Spirit is presently very much at work in believing people and in the Church?

One such sign is the Second Vatican Council. Another is ecumenism. Another is liturgical reform. Another is the new openness and freedom in the Church, and even the

fierce controversy thus aroused. Another is the evident
hunger for personal contact with God, for unvarnished
and even painful truth, for evangelical virtue, for authentic prayer.

Not trifling marks, these, of the urging presence of the
Holy Spirit.

The Two Commandments

*Jesus asked him: What is it that is written in the law? . . .
And he answered: You shall love the Lord your God with
the love of your whole heart, and your whole soul, and
your whole strength, and your whole mind; and your
neighbor as yourself. You have answered right, he told
him; do this, and you will find life.* (Luke 10:26–28; Gospel of the Twelfth Sunday after Pentecost)

In the second liturgical reading of this Sunday, Christ our
Redeemer and Teacher, asked about the path to eternal
life, answers: *What is it that is written in the law?* Then,
without adding a word of His own, He approves a formula made up of combined quotations from Deuteronomy
and Leviticus. Our Lord's two great commandments come,
word for word, from the Old Law.

It might not be ill advised to draw an immediate moral.
The point is evident enough, but present circumstances

urge that it be rehearsed. Everything was not wrong before Christ, everything has not been right since. What is more —of more immediate concern, at least—everything in the Church was not wrong before Vatican II, and everything has not been infallibly and irreproachably right since.

The commonplace observation should not be read as a complaint. Everyone understands that the Church continues to plod and stumble along her pilgrim way through what indisputably continues to be a valley of tears. The Promised Land may be nearer than it was; but it is not near.

A particular trend that is noticeable in the Church of today as distinct from the Church of yesterday is the shift in emphasis from the first to the second of the two great commandments. No one is suggesting that for the Christian the love of God no longer matters; no one of a Christian mind is attempting to divorce the love of neighbor from the love of God. Nevertheless, the contemporary Church manifestly takes much to heart and conscience the argument of the first Johannine letter: *If a man boasts of loving God, while he hates* (read *neglects*) *his own brother, he is a liar. He has seen his brother, and has no love for him; what love can he have for the God he has never seen?* Increasingly, Christian love of God is being seen, interpreted and implemented as service of man. The religious man of another time is blamed for straining his interior vision in order to catch a glimpse of God in high heaven, while he seemed unable to see the poor and hungry fellow on his doorstep.

The beloved parable that we hear again today from the Lord Christ insures that the new awakening of the

Christian conscience to immediate and practical concern for that very real neighbor who stands in dire need cannot constitute a mistake in direction for the contemporary Church. There can be no harm, however, in repeating an observation that has been made before. The Christian, sincerely and rightly intent on service out of love for neighbor, will not therefore neglect personal prayer and self-discipline out of love for God. The great commandments continue to be two, not one.

Reward and Promise

I established myself, then, in Sion, coming to rest obediently in the holy city; Jerusalem should be my domain. Deeply I struck root among a privileged nation, God granting me my lot in his own chosen territory; mine to abide in the company of his faithful servants. (Ecclesiastes 25:15–16; Epistle of the Feast of the Assumption)

The speaker in the first liturgical reading of Assumption day is Wisdom personified. As the Scripture scholars have made clear to us, the Wisdom motif, prominent almost throughout the Old Testament, underwent a steady and remarkable evolution in the hands of the inspired authors. Beginning as the "result of mere human experience as assessed by the work of human reflection" (Louis Bouyer),

Wisdom, through the mediation of the notion that only God is truly wise, is finally apotheosized by the writers of Israel: "Wisdom is for God like another self."

What is even more striking is the identification, early in the Christian era, of Wisdom with Mary, the Mother of Christ. The identification is not made in the New Testament; it is the work of the young Church. Again we quote Fr. Bouyer: "What is perhaps most remarkable about this application to Mary of the Wisdom texts is the spontaneous manner in which it seems to have occurred. No great Doctor can be named as having proposed it; but liturgies of both East and West give evidence of what we might call a tacit understanding, a universal instinct, not the outcome of intellectual speculation but giving rise to it." The noted scholar adds an engaging observation: "The Russian Church has a special office of Sancta Sophia (Holy Wisdom), which is celebrated conjointly with that of the Assumption."

We cannot do better than allow Fr. Bouyer to explain to us the significance of the Mary-Wisdom theme: "What emerges from these liturgical evidences is that the Church sees our Lady as the predestinated par excellence, on whom the divine Wisdom comes down to make of her a first created realization of himself, one that contains already, as it were in material fashion, his final realization in the new creature, the Church at the end of time, the entire assembly of the predestined."

It amounts to a commonplace, then, to say that the Assumption is a strongly eschatological celebration; but here is a commonplace that wants fresh consideration.

The Assumption of our Lady into joy and glory, this

unique, God-given and perfect triumph over the diabolical sin-death-hell triumvirate, is both reward and pledge. It is Mary's final reward for her all-inclusive yes to God at the critical moment of her life. It is her vaulting recompense (if we may take a hint from this day's Gospel reading) for her unwavering choice, in loving faith, of the invisible over the visible, the supernatural over the natural, the ultimate over the immediate, the will and wisdom of God over the inclination and prudence of man.

Further, the Assumption of Mary, like the resurrection of her Son, stands as a radiant pledge of the ultimate state of the man of faith, when there shall occur divine Wisdom's "final realization in the new creature, the Church at the end of time, the entire assembly of the predestined."

In view of that free cooperation of Mary with grace which is so underscored by Luke's account of the Annunciation and so strongly implied by John's account of the crucifixion, no reasonable Christian will stumble over or gamble on that word "predestined." Salvation is a mystery, but let no one presume that the robe of glory is a prefitted garment. God helping, our Lady interceding, we must shape ourselves for it.

Leprosy, Priests and Gratefulness

Jesus answered, Were not all ten made clean? And the other nine, where are they? Not one has come back to give God the praise, except this stranger. (Luke 17:17–18; Gospel of the Thirteenth Sunday after Pentecost)

Today's brief Gospel is ideally lucid. The forthright story of the lepers unfailingly prompts various trains of thought in the reflective Christian mind.

The miracle of the Gospel is another of those beneficent wonders of healing with which the synoptic narratives abound, but in this instance there are two particular points that merit notice.

Leprosy was one of the special horrors of the ancient world. There existed no method of coping with the disease in any medical or curative way. Most terrifying, of course, was the infectious character of leprosy. The victim was simply and straightway banished from human society, and that was the end of the matter. Because the visible effects of the dreadful malady were so ghastly, leprosy was regarded not only as a degeneration of the body, but as a corruption and defilement of the entire human person. In the Gospels all other sicknesses are *cured;* the leper is *made clean.* Small wonder that early commentators like St. Augustine saw in Christ's healing of lepers a symbol of the cleansing of souls infected with heresy or defiled by grave sin.

Notable also in this evangelical account is the unusual detail that our Saviour does not immediately and personally heal the lepers. He does not touch them or even, it would seem, approach them: they *stood far off, crying aloud, Jesus, master, have pity on us.* We then read that *He met them with the words, Go and show yourselves to the priests.* The miracle took place as the lepers obeyed this directive. *And thereupon, as they went, they were made clean.* Again, it is understandable that the classical Gospel commentators found here an apt symbol of the sacrament of penance.

In all the current ferment about the priest-layman relationship in the Church, it might not be idle to recall that the true position and special powers of the priest are neither administrative nor sociological, nor even primarily of the intellectual order, but sacramental. Being what he is by virtue of a sacrament, the priest is the ordinary minister of baptism; he is empowered to forgive sin; he makes Christ present in the Eucharist; he solemnizes Christian marriage; with cleansing and maybe healing oil he anoints the sick. If now the priest is derided for doing badly what the layman does or could do well, perhaps— setting aside the mocking malevolence of some few critics —no particular harm is done. If everyone wants the priest to be a priest, he will be the first to rejoice in a limitation and assignment that he desired in the first place.

The final and most evident suggestion of this Gospel reading is, of course, the seemliness of gratitude to God for blessings received, a gratitude that will be not only keenly and habitually felt, but openly and habitually expressed. We must notice that here is one of the Gospel passages in which our Saviour flatly declares Himself disappointed in people. In general, our Lord was resolutely optimistic about human beings. He set exceedingly high standards—*But you are to be perfect, as your heavenly Father is perfect*—and did so with complete seriousness. He cannot but be pained, therefore, when we take all His benefits, take them greedily, and take them for granted.

Temporary Rain and Fog

It is for the heathen to busy themselves over such things; you have a Father in heaven who knows that you need them all. Make it your first care to find the kingdom of God, and his approval, and all these things shall be yours without asking. (Matthew 6:32–33; Gospel of the Fourteenth Sunday after Pentecost)

The major blessing bestowed by an all-loving Creator upon the beast is that the animal lives exclusively in the moment. Animals do have rudimentary memory, and a bird does build a nest for its coming young, a squirrel does gather food against the winter; but recollection seems not to agitate the animal, and the bird and the squirrel don't *worry* whether the nest will be adequate or the winter severe.

Man, on the contrary, cannot live totally or easily in the moment. He remembers the past, sometimes joyfully, often with exquisite pain. He constantly, vividly anticipates the future. Nor is man to be blamed for his sharp self-awareness, his remembrance of his intimate history, his busy scanning of the veiled future. He wants to know who he is. He is keen to know the meaning of what he has already done or experienced. Above all, he must know where he is headed and how he can get there.

In the moving Gospel passage we hear today, Christ our Lord—*Christ the power of God, Christ the wisdom of God*—eloquently warns His followers against undue anxiety about the future. Specifically, He condemns worry about future material needs, deliberately choosing for His examples of unconcern the two needs which for every man are most urgent: food and clothing. Surprising as it may seem, our Lord says flatly that it is un-Christian to worry about such necessities. *You have a Father in heaven who knows that you need them all.*

It is by no means fanciful to suggest that the contemporary Christian, but particularly the contemporary Catholic, is apt to be suffering a different kind of anxiety about what lies ahead. This man is worried about his religious future. He is not to be blamed for this uneasiness, either. Deprived of his comfortable certainties and shaken in his familiar pieties, seeing the beloved image of his Church now cracked and stained, directed to estimate moral and religious values by new and alarmingly flexible standards, our good man of faith wonders indeed and increasingly about the religious future into which he and his children are stumbling. He is not certain as to what his immediate religious destination ought to be, he is not at all certain that he would want it if he knew it.

The thoughtful contemporary Catholic is not lost, exactly. It's just that the road map has been called in for revision, and the car itself (a perfectly good make) stands in need of safety devices. Our man must simply inch his way carefully along the pilgrim road. Unfortunately, it is raining, and there are patches of fog.

Yet Christ our Lord is on record with the repeated counsel: *Do not fret.* If Christ said that about food and clothing, He certainly says it now about faith and the Church. If, with regard to the essential supports of material life, *you have a Father in heaven who knows that you need them all* and who will somehow supply them, it must be true that our loving and attentive Father will continue to impart both to the Church and to the individual believer that mighty Spirit who, in keeping with the promise of Christ, will *guide you into all truth.*

It would be fun (if not a shock) to know what the Christians of 2067 will be thinking and saying about their ancestors of 1967. For us, by that time, the rain will have ceased, the fog lifted, and the road map will be quite unnecessary.

Spiritual Death?

And just as he draw near the gate of the city, a dead man was being carried out to his burial; the only son of his mother, and she was a widow. (Luke 7:12; Gospel of the Fifteenth Sunday after Pentecost)

On the strength of our Lord's own recorded use of Scripture and with the countenance of of St. Paul's dictum that an event set down in Scripture can be *a symbol*, the record of which was *written as a warning to us.* Christian writers and speakers have never hesitated to draw a secondary meaning from passages in the inspired Word of God. What these commentators were about was perfectly clear: they were "applying" the scriptural testimony to a current situation, thereby suggesting a moral lesson. The strictly *ad hoc* procedure, not pretending to be anything more, was both reasonable and constructive.

So the vivid, touching narrative we hear again today, a story of physical death and, by the mercy and might of Christ, return to physical life, was seen as a symbol of spiritual death and return to spiritual life. The parallelism rested on the conviction that a person's spiritual situation, like his physical, is not a merely static or technical or juridical affair, but involves a dynamism that constitutes a genuine "life." When a man walks obediently in friendship with God, he possesses the interior reality of sanctifying grace; he is spiritually—but by no means only metaphorically—"alive." If a man gravely disobeys God's law, if he knowingly, willfully opts for serious moral evils, then he is interiorly alienated from God, he is spiritually "dead."

In a time of sophisticated speculation on every aspect of Christian belief and practice, does this talk of supernatural life and death sound naïve? Is the whole analogy merely picturesque, or does it express a reality of the highest consequence?

It is just, as well as somewhat overdue, that responsible guides should insist that the Christian way is one of love rather than law. It is proper to reexamine the credentials of various religious and moral obligations, asking whether (for one thing) they are of God or of man. It is reasonable, when told that this or that mandate binds the conscience under pain of grave sin, to inquire into the evidence for such a grievous declaration. It is salutary to point out that what appears to be a free and chosen act is, upon occasion and under circumstances, no such thing. It is prudent, by and large, to suspect that spiritual death is not actually as epidemic as immediately indications might suggest.

When all these handsome and soothing concessions have been made, we are left with a small collection of truths so obvious that they can only be expressed as platitudes. God, with every right, forbids what is evil and commands what is good. Man, who owes all to God, who depends on God for every breath he draws, is bound in conscience to heed God's commands. Man is radically, normally free, truly free, to obey God or to disobey Him. Choosing to disobey

God in a grave matter, man thereby sets himself up in opposition to God, and thus in an authentic sense *separates* himself from God. But God, who *is,* is life. Separation from God is death.

Christian instructors do ill to exaggerate either the incidence or the gravity of real moral evil. Currently, the danger of such exaggeration seems minimal. The trend might be rather to think away sin, to talk away sin, to wish away sin—possibly without avoiding sin.

Hand and Heart

Jesus asked the lawyers and Pharisees openly: Is healing allowed on the sabbath day? Then, as they did not answer, he took the man by the hand, and sent him away healed. (Luke 14:3–4; Gospel of the Sixteenth Sunday after Pentecost)

The heart, which in the physical order is simply a major muscle in the body, is the symbol of interior spirit or attitude. The hand (the raised arm, the clenched fist) is the symbol of fact or deed. Everyone is quite aware of the distinction in question. We say easily of an unwelcome chore: "My heart isn't in it."

As is evident in the Gospel reading of this day, the issue of his visible deed plus or minus interior spirit has always made a critical problem in religion. Our Lord, in particular, vigorously attacked the problem in various ways on various occasions. In our present day, as an entire generation advances toward maturity in avowed detestation of the appearance that belies the actuality (*phony* is the current word), the issue of personal and institutional authenticity in religion draws more and more attention, disturbs more and more people of faith.

It goes without saying that in all significant human activity the heart and the hand ought to work together in the relationship of cause and effect. A cause produces a characteristic and proportionate effect. Of certain laboring heroes faced with a prodigious rowing task old Virgil remarked: *Possunt quia posse videntur,* which could be rendered: "They can do it because they think they can." People who simply will not desist from putting one foot in front of the other, at whatever cost, will somehow and ultimately arrive at their destination. It is when this relationship of cause and effect is dislocated that the problem of authenticity arises.

One variant of such dislocation is the presence of spirit and the absence of deed. Instantly we perceive a situation that is either untruthful—the alleged interior spirit is actually not present—or so futile and unproductive as to be meaningless.

Much more troublesome is the spiritless deed, that deceptive phenomenon which contemporary feeling finds so revolting. Here, first, is the visible act that is performed without heart in the sense that it is done almost without mind: ritually, mechanically, automatically. The deed is done, but it is hollow. Such interior absence of the person from the act, however unintended that absence may be, is surely the primary reason for the distaste not a few Catholics feel for the rosary.

Worse yet is the act that is heartless in a far more destructive sense: the deed is performed out of policy, for observation or the record, in the interest of personal or institutional advantage of one kind or another. The action is not only spiritless (though it may be spirited enough) in that it flows from no religious or "pure" motivation, but also in the irreligious sense that it knowingly implies an interior spirit or belief or conviction that is not present. In short, the action is a pretense and therefore an ultimate lie. To proclaim the religious value of poverty while living in unfailing, cultivated affluence will presently exercise a disillusioning effect on the majority of observers.

"Hypocrite" is an ugly word for an ugly thing—a word Christ our Lord did not hesitate to apply (as in Matthew 23, where it occurs seven times) to men whose seemingly religious deeds were inspired and informed by no religious spirit. The desire of our time for religion that is not merely technical or mechanical or legalistic is sound. *God is a spirit,* our Saviour said to that remarkable Samaritan woman, *and those who worship him must worship him in spirit and in truth.* Christianity is not mere activity, not a religion of the visible hand rather than of the unseen heart. In religion as in health, heart-failure can be fatal.

Two Commandments and a Question

Then, while the Pharisees were still gathered about him, Jesus asked them: What is your opinion concerning Christ? Whose son is he said to be? (Matthew 22:41–42; Gospel of the Seventeenth Sunday after Pentecost)

A comparison of the two liturgical readings of this Sunday might provide an apt commentary on a leading religious issue of our time.

The brief excerpt from the Pauline letter to the Christians of Ephesus urges, in terms that can scarcely be bettered, the cause of *that unity the Spirit gives* to all who believe in Christ. *You are one body, with a single Spirit; each of you, when he was called, called in the same hope; with the same Lord, the same faith, the same baptism; with the same God, the same Father, all of us.* Brief as the appeal is, it is powerful. The immediate reaction of the Christian reader or hearer might well be: Linked together by such strong bonds, how can we possibly be riven one from another?

It is perhaps the highest religious credit of the period in which we live that division, with its constant threat of hostility, among men of faith—and especially among men who adhere to *the same Lord* Christ—is acknowledged to be not only surprising, but a scandal. Christian leaders

strive as they have not striven in four centuries and more
to end the scandal by healing, so far as may be at any moment, the breach between their peoples. The concerted
effort toward unity is clearly much more than a movement
of politeness or policy. It is a perfectly genuine thrust, inspired by the Holy Spirit and rooted in deep Christian
religious convictions. Already the ecumenical enterprise
has been more fruitful than the most sanguine observer
would have prophesied 25 years ago, and reasonable pros-
pects for the future range from fair to brilliant.

Now turn to the Gospel that is read today. The Saviour
is enmeshed in controversy. In answer to *a question* put
to try him, Christ lays down as the basic imperatives of
His religious system the twin principles of love of God
and love of neighbor, which cannot be faulted by Christian or Jew or any man of any faith. Yet divisive controversy
breaks out, and breaks out over a query posed by the
Saviour Himself. The fact is impressive. Our Lord, whose
solemn prayer for unity is now so often and so justly
quoted, would be the last to raise a divisive issue unless
ultimate values were at stake.

So, then, even as we all long for and labor toward
Christian unity, we must together and boldly and honestly
face the question proposed: *What is your opinion concerning Christ? Whose son is he to be?*

The varying Christian answers given to this decisive
Christian question must not occasion discouragement in
the pursuit of Christian unity. Here, as in every other
issue that divides us, we must continue to reflect, discuss
and even to argue. There is ever lessening risk of estrangement and bitterness in ecumenical debate. A new factor

has appeared in religious discussion, a factor that unhappily was lost either 400 or 2,000 years ago. That element is sincere respect for the religious opposite number. We've learned at last what we unaccountably have long overlooked: that the discussion or argument about *opinion concerning* Christ must be conducted against the background of *the greatest of the commandments* and *the second, its like:* love of God, love of neighbor.

Like everything else that is both delicate and valuable, the ecumenical encounter wants careful handling. To vary the metaphor, the run for religious unity is a steeplechase over high obstacles, and the hotheads and the rough riders must be gradually disqualified by the responsible stewards.

Sin and Forgiveness

And now they brought before him a man who was palsied and bedridden; whereupon Jesus, seeing their faith, said to the palsied man: Son, take courage, your sins are forgiven. (Matthew 9:2; Gospel of the Eighteenth Sunday after Pentecost)

The fact is that Christ our Saviour, who often in the Gospels speaks of the forgiveness of sin, is represented by all

four Evangelists as actually forgiving sin. The fact is
worthy of more than passing notice.

Most obviously, if Christ personally and explicitly forgave sin, He assumed the actuality of sin. It is not easy to
suppose that the Saviour on repeated occasions performed
a therapeutic ceremony that had no real content. If He
forgave sin, there was sin to be forgiven. One would feel
foolish to be making such an evident point were it not for
a certain mood that appears to be resulting from present
discussions, both religious and psychological, of moral responsibility. The mood is one of most determined optimism. The optimist view is that man is a decent sort,
really, even though some of his choices are smelly, cruel,
destructive and brazenly self-seeking. Has anyone noticed
that the terms "sin" and "sinner" are increasingly absent
from religious speaking and writing? At any rate, Christ
our Lord forgave sin. He did something real about something real.

Jewish tradition, here backed up by plain logic, firmly
regarded the forgiveness of sin as strictly a divine preroga-
tive. One of the splendid Judaic clarities was that sin,
whatever its social implications, was an offense against
God. Therefore only God could forgive sin. When Christ
forgave sin, the obvious challenge was immediately thrown
up to Him. He welcomes the challenge, performs a miracle to demonstrate His contention. Only God can forgive
sin. But Christ forgives sin. *Ergo* . . .

In this extremely important connection another fact is
recorded in the Gospels—or rather, in a single verse of
one Gospel, though the brief passage is not without evangelical parallels. According to St. John, Christ on the

evening of His resurrection said to His disciples: *Receive the Holy Spirit; when you forgive men's sins, they are forgiven; when you hold them bound, they are held bound.* The additional fact, then: Christ delegated the power to forgive sin.

Surely it is not polemical to suggest the immense and immediate consolation for religious man of being able to turn to some living, accessible and accredited person for actual forgiveness of actual sin.

Of course, there is the drawback, in the tradition of auricular confession, of literal and specific self-revelation to another man like oneself. The process is not easy for anyone, it is agony for the proud spirit whose image is dearer to him than his reality. Here we encounter one of the serious dangers involved in the heady, optimist view of moral behavior. Not a few Catholics, if they can convince themselves that they need not go to confession, will not go. They will thus be deprived of the very considerable benefits that attach to the regular use of a sacrament; a sacrament, mind; not a sacramental or an oppressive form of bureaucratic red tape.

Decline in Catholic attachment to a sacrament would make an odd kind of aggiornamento.

Invitation Requires Answer

After this, he said to his servants: Here is the marriage feast all ready, and those who had been invited have proved unworthy of it. You must go out to the street corners, and invite all whom you find there to the wedding. (Matthew 22:8–9; Gospel of the Nineteenth Sunday after Pentecost)

The nuptial image for the appointed relationship between God and man is by no means a Christian invention. The idea of God as a lover and Israel as the tarnished yet beloved bride occurs in the Old Testament. Commentators have observed that the Saviour, as He is quoted by the Evangelists, makes only a single explicit reference to Himself as bridegroom, but the image is strongly indicated in His repeated use of the wedding-feast parable. The picture is not only powerfully appealing but also squarely didactic. The essential characteristic of the relationship between God and man is, or ought to be, love, and the goal of that relationship is intimate, joyous, indissoluble union.

As is evident from our Saviour's present story of the *king who held a marriage feast for his son,* the desired relationship between God and man does not occur and flower automatically. Take it or leave it, God's large plan in His dealings with mankind called for a divine entry or intervention in human history at a particular time and place, the divine overture being made to a particular and chosen people. When this people had, according to plan, lovingly responded to God's loving invitation, it would then become their duty and privilege to carry the word of the divine love to the whole world.

The painful point of our Lord's story is the failure of beloved Israel to respond to the divine call. Often, as the Old Testament makes abundantly clear, had Israel the bride proved unfaithful to God her lover. Always God had forgiven the infidelity, always had Israel been welcomed back to pure nuptial love. The supreme test, which would be embodied in the advent of the Messiah, was yet to come. At last there appears a man of Nazareth in Galilee—despised *Galilee of the gentiles*—a man of plain parentage and simple ways, yet a man clearly possessed of extraordinary prophetic and miraculous powers. This Jesus declares: "I am He, the Christ, the Messiah. I am the Bridegroom."

The Bridegroom is rejected. What, then? The parable answers: the rejected Christ will turn to the gentiles. The divine invitation will be extended, and with vigor, to the unprivileged *goyim*.

As is clear from the Acts of the Apostles, this sore problem of the relationship of the nascent Church to the gentile world was the first and most perilous crisis for Christianity. It is no blame to say of ancient Judaism that it constituted a closed and exclusive society. Only thus— and even so, it was a near thing—could Israel be preserved from polytheistic contamination. What we can scarcely appreciate today is the shock to the original Jewish Christians when the Church, through Paul, announced and implemented the mystery of universal salvation. Only then were some of the remembered sayings and parables of Christ finally understood.

Of course, the vocation of the gentiles wasn't automatic, either; that is the meaning, in the story, of the curious coda about the guest who appeared at the wedding without proper garb. The entire parable rehearses the crucial truth that Christ our Lord expounded in so many ways. God is love; God offers love; but love demands mutuality, response, love-in-return. Sooner or later, somehow or other, man, every man, must answer God who says: "I love you."

St. John and Faith

Sir, the nobleman said to him, come down before my child dies. Go back home, Jesus told him, thy son is to live. And the man began his journey home, putting his trust in the words Jesus had spoken to him. (John 4:49–50; Gospel of the Twentieth Sunday after Pentecost)

John the Evangelist, as has always been suspected and is now clearly appreciated, is an exceedingly subtle writer. It is sometimes difficult to say with certainty what element in a narrative is uppermost or at least prominent in John's

mind. In the case of our present miracle, John draws attention to the fact that it took place at Cana, the scene of the
first miracle recorded in the fourth Gospel. When one
compares the two narratives, the really significant factor
emerges. It is not locale, but the decisive question of complete faith in the words and deeds of Jesus of Nazareth.
The whole phenomenon or issue of faith is, of course, one
of the leading ideas in the Johannine witness.

There are several points stressed by John in connection
with faith.

First and most obviously, John is concerned not simply
with faith in a divine Being, in the God of Abraham,
Isaac and Jacob, but with faith in Jesus of Nazareth. As
has often been remarked, the fourth Gospel is the record
and transmission of a powerful personal experience of
encounter with Christ. This Gospel has a far more personal and intimate quality than the witness of the Synoptics, and the purpose of the writer is specified from
beginning to end: *that you may learn to believe that
Jesus is the Christ, the Son of God, and so believing find
life through his name.* The *life* that John constantly
promises his readers is altogether contingent on faith in
the man Jesus.

Next, John is most painfully aware that this faith in
Christ can be refused. Again from beginning to end, his
Gospel is a testimony to the sad fact that men did refuse
such faith. So there is in faith a free, volitional element;
and John is surprisingly severe on those who will not
make this act of faith in the Lord, whose credentials, in
John's eyes, are irresistible. The Evangelist's explanation
of the situation is uncompromising: *when the light came*

into the world men preferred darkness to light; preferred it, because their doings were evil. Perhaps we of a later time are more puzzled, in our dubious sophistication, by the mystery of faith than was John; and, of course, we have not experienced Christ as he did. At any rate, modern views on responsibility for lack of faith tend to be tolerant. No one wishes to turn back the clock, but John's inspired observations on this as on other subjects are worthy of some notice.

Lastly, John's narratives stressing the connection between the signs wrought by Christ and consequent—or, as in the present instance, *antecedent*—faith in Christ indicate that John is fully aware of a particular element in the act of faith. That element can be described only as a kind of blindness or even recklessness. It is patent that when the demonstration of a fact or proposition totally excludes all possibility of doubt, we may indeed speak of resultant conviction or certainty, but there is no longer any question of faith. One recalls with wry amusement the character in *Father Malachy's Miracle* who only wanted a photograph of the Holy Spirit. No doubt, when men believe religiously, and especially when they make sacrifices for their belief, they are running a certain risk. The same is true—emphatically so—of those who, in John's language, refuse belief.

The story of the nobleman's son has a happy ending. The reason for the happy ending is, evidently, a strong, blind faith in *Jesus . . . the Christ, the Son of God.* On the same grounds, and with remarkable confidence, many of us look for a happy ending to our lives.

A : B = B : C

Then the master sent for him. You wicked servant, he said, I forgave you the whole of that debt because you pleaded with me. Was it not your duty also to have mercy on your fellow servant as I had mercy on you? (Matthew 18:32–33; Gospel of the Twenty-First Sunday after Pentecost)

Unsurprisingly, Msgr. Knox of treasured memory makes a keen observation in connection with our present Gospel reading. As the parable of the unforgiving servant is as clear and satisfying as any of our Lord's short stories, so the parable of the embezzling steward (Eighth Sunday after Pentecost) is the most perplexing; yet the two tales share a common general theme. The theme is familiar, for in one way or another Christ our Lord rehearsed it assiduously: the relationship between God and man is conditioned by the relationship between man and man. The situation could be described in the broad terms of a mathematical proportion. God will act toward man as man acts toward his fellow man.

One of the paradoxes that mark the mortal life of the human being is that he cannot and indeed does not wish to get along without other men, yet finds it so exceedingly difficult to get along *with* them. It is obvious that man is, by the whole force of his nature, social. It is equally

obvious that man is consistently antisocial in the sense that
he regularly acts in destructive hostility toward other men.

The lengthy catalogue of reasons for antisocial behavior
is reducible, of course, to one reason, and that is the instinctive, deep-rooted, incorrigible self-regard with which
each one of us is born and with which we must live and
struggle throughout life. It must never be forgotten how
both the Old Testament and Christ Himself express the
obligation of love between man and man. *Thou shalt love
thy neighbor as thyself.* Self-love is not praised, but it is
not denied. It is treated as a datum.

The problem is clearly that of control. How can the
human person be motivated to moderate that self-seeking
which appears to him so natural and indeed so necessary?
Is it not right that the leaders and teachers of men, in
addition to proclaiming the loftiest motives for generous
and noble behavior, should also urge that unlimited self-
interest is also destructive of the best interests of the self?

The Old Testament is unembarrassed in its frequent
appeal for religious observance and moral rectitude on the
ground that thus it will be well, here and now, with a
man. Christ our Saviour, even as He announced the purest
and most exalted code of thought and action, did not hesitate to speak also of reward and punishment in consequence of men's deeds. Thus in our present parable, after
the cruel servant has been handed over to the torturers,
Christ warns: *That is how my heavenly Father will deal
with you unless you each forgive your brother from your
heart.* In the Sermon on the Mount, we read the epigram
that popular Christian tradition has named the Golden
Rule: *Treat others as you would have others treat you.*

Thousands of times every day, Christians throughout the world repeat with understandable yet astonishing inattention: *Forgive us our trespasses as we forgive those who trespass against us.*

It is not easy to attract mortal men, burdened as they are with the legacy of original sin, to consistent action that is informed with the highest principles. It is not easy to persuade men in all their hungers that when they diminish another man they diminish themselves. We Christians are quite familiar with the powerful, wide-ranging teachings and exhortations of Christ Himself; and how responsive are we? Still—we can always listen again, and reflect again, and ask help again, and try again.

The Facts of the Matter

He [Christ] *is the true likeness of the God we cannot see; his is that first birth which precedes every act of creation. Yes, in him all created things took their being. . . . He takes precedency of all, in him all subsist.* (Colossians 1:15–17; Epistle of the Feast of Christ the King)

Amid the clamor of controversy on so many religious issues, the liturgical festival of Christ the King comes as a most welcome reassurance. Even while startling questions are being asked in dynamic theology about the

Saviour Himself, the Christian mind and heart may rest secure in unassailable certainties about Jesus of Nazareth.

For example, Christ is a fact—an objective, historical reality. Jesus of Nazareth, as His name declares, appeared on this earth at a definite time, in a particular place, born of a mother whom people knew well, child of a specific nationality and culture. He bore an individual appearance (of which we know simply nothing); He was of a determined weight and height; He manifestly had strong convictions and feelings. In a word, He was a man.

A second solid fact about Jesus of Nazareth is that He is an object of faith. At first glance it might seem that what we meet here is by no means a certainty, but, rather, a large uncertainty. Not so. *What* each man will believe about Christ is indeed a question; but each man will believe *something* about Christ. If an individual contends that Jesus of Nazareth was a man and nothing more, Christ is the object of faith denied. It is the old story: you can take Christ or leave Him, but you cannot ignore Him.

Historic Christian faith believes that Jesus of Nazareth was and is God. *My Father and I are one,* says the Saviour in the fourth Gospel. *His nature is, from the first, divine,* writes St. Paul of Christ. The Epistle to the Hebrews describes Him as the *Son, who is the radiance of the Father's splendor, and the full expression of his being.* It may be that, as time passes and the tools that are words become blunted and therefore less useful, Christian faith will be less inclined to use terms like *nature* and *person* in speaking of Christ. No matter. Christian faith will know and say, in whatever symbols, that Jesus is God.

A third indisputable fact about Christ is that He is an object of love.

Love is the "in" word in contemporary Christianity. Very good. Much more often than not, the word is employed in its social or global connotation of love of man for man, and extensive, strongly activist conclusions are drawn from the religious imperative of love of neighbor. Again, very good. Only, let the first Christian love be not forgotten, nor for a moment be obscured or dulled. No doubt it would be somewhat lacking in taste if Christian pickets or demonstrators carried signs reading: "We Love the Lord Christ." On the other hand, it shouldn't be necessary.

We must all have a faith-full and intimate word, this day, with King Jesus.

The Promised End

The souls of the just are in God's hand, and tormenting malice will not touch them. In the eyes of fools the just appeared to die; but they are at peace. (Wisdom 3:1–3; Offertory Verse of the Mass of All Saints)

Throughout the year, the Church celebrates the memory, and more than the memory, of this good man and that fine woman whom she lists in her calendar of saints. On the first day of November, the Church holds festival for the

entire army of saints: all whom she has not saluted in-
dividually, all whom she does not even know by name,
whose heroic virtue is known only to God.

This liturgical observance cannot but raise questions in
a sincerely ecumenical age. All Hallows (as the day used to
be called) involves the doctrine of the intercession of
saints. The intercession of saints involves the doctrine of
the communion of saints. The communion of saints involves the doctrine of purgatory. On more than one count,
consequently, All Hallows points up an ecumenical problem.

Are doctrines such as these strictly scriptural, are they
to be found with any explicitation in New Testament
theology? With this tangled question the present commentator is simply not competent to deal. We will be content to inquire briefly into the intrinsic reasonableness of
the basic ideas contained in these teachings.

The notion of purification is one of those profound and
pervasive intuitions that are to be found in every religious
system worthy of the name. Man and God are not peers.
If man is really to know God, if, above all, man is ever to
possess God, man must be geared or shaped or conditioned for a situation, a state of being, that is flatly beyond
his natural capacity. In a word, man must be *purified* for
his final, personal encounter and union with God. The
Catholic doctrine of purgatory means simply that the
process of purification, if not completed in this life, can
and will be continued after death.

What is called the *communion of saints* embodies the
idea, demonstrably present in the recorded teaching of
Christ, that the Church is one. The Church, as everyone

keeps repeating nowadays, is both a present and an eschatological reality. Its true dimensions extend beyond the space and time and state of this world. Yet there is but one Church; one Church comprised of three branches or stages of growth.

All those members of Christ who are now finally with God make up the Church Triumphant. Those who, having completed their mortal lives, are yet completing their purification are the Church Suffering. Those of us who still draw breath and who labor daily toward the promised end constitute the Church Militant. Since the Church is one, would it not seem fitting that the Church Militant, with the means at is disposal, should be able to help the Church Suffering, and that the Church Triumphant, from its place of advantage, should succor the Church Militant? Why must the incident of death terminate the loving assistance that the members of Christ's Body, by prayer and sacrifice, most certainly lend one another in this life?

We will, of course, dutifully repeat the truism that anything, however good and sound, can become distorted or exaggerated with the passage of time—especially on the popular level. The cult of saints has indeed been exaggerated, invariably with a view to miraculous powers of intercession, and often enough to the detriment of the most essential Catholic practices. The supposed torments of the souls in purgatory have indeed provided many a hearty preacher with an emotional and durable theme. Too bad. But on the first two days of each November, Mother Church will continue to recall and celebrate not fable but fact, not rhetoric but reality.

The Christian Citizen

So they brought him a silver piece, and he asked them: Whose is this likeness? Whose name is inscribed on it? Caesar's, they said; whereupon he answered: Why then, give back to Caesar what is Caesar's, and to God what is God's. (Matthew 22:19–21; Gospel of the Twenty-Second Sunday after Pentecost)

Christianity, originally proscribed as the deadly enemy of the state, in three centuries became the partner of the state. The first situation was murderous, the second turned out to be both seductive and misleading. Western man now seems to have concluded with a certain finality that a general policy of separation together with cooperation is, in the long haul, best for both Church and State. Problems remain, of course, since it is the same man who is *homo religiosus* and *homo politicus,* and his two urgent interests do not inevitably march together.

The Christian of the free world will not cease to be grateful for authentic religious freedom. Such liberty is indeed a right and not a favor, but it is a right that so often in history—as in too many places today—has been brutally denied. It is not beyond understanding that Caesar is not always at ease with God, for religion is a force at once powerful and paradoxical. Religion enlight-

ens men and blinds them, it quiets them and maddens
them, it can make them wash another's feet or remove his
head. Besides, when Caesar comes into conflict with God,
against all appearances God has a way of coming out on
top. The American Christian will therefore be honestly
grateful for the record and the persevering stance of his
country in the matter of religious freedom.

It follows that the man of faith will, with particular
reason, discharge in all fidelity the duties of the good citizen. True it is that a man's religious beliefs will not always
solve the complex problems that the citizen, as citizen,
must face. Religion does not unequivocally answer the
question of Vietnam or the question of munition sales or
the question of the national debt ceiling, and religion
must not normally suggest a preference for one political
party over another. Yet there are situations and there are
issues—the matter of social justice, for example—in which
religious conviction should strongly enforce the demands
of enlightened citizenship. It is distressing that sometimes
honest citizenship will make a man truly religious, in practice, toward his fellow man, while religion may fail to
reciprocate.

Just as the state ought to be able to look to the Christian, as Christian, for reasonable support, so the Christian,
as Christian, may expect reasonable and unspecial assistance from the state. The Catholic, in particular, will
decline to be embarrassed by the peculiar outcry that
greets his efforts to secure needed and modest aid for a
creditable school system—one that constitutes, in simple
fact, an immense boon to the state. It is an enviable characteristic of our Jewish brothers that they unhesitatingly

and openly and most vigorously seek every kind of support from every quarter for Jewish concerns all over the world. The committed Catholic is no less a good citizen—on the contrary—if he lobbies unashamedly for a degree of co-operation, for the common good, between Church and State, a degree of cooperation that scarcely resembles or threatens the establishment of a state religion.

Today's Gospel gives us our Lord's only recorded comment on Church and State. Christ is no disturber of the civil peace. He is perfectly willing to cooperate honorably with Caesar. Let Caesar cooperate reasonably with Him.

Where Angels Fear to Tread

Jesus turned and caught sight of her; and he said: Have no fear, my daughter, your faith has brought you healing. . . . But when the multitude had been turned away, he went in and took the girl by the hand, and she rose up. (Matthew 9:22, 25; Gospel for the Twenty-Third Sunday after Pentecost)

For evident reasons, the evangelical excerpt that we read today has been called a "women's Gospel." Straightway one begins to think of the somewhat agitated question of the place and function of women in the modernized Christian Church. Should women be more articulate and more directly influential in the world of institutional religion? Should women, religious and lay, have a deliberate voice in an ecumenical council? Should women be ordained priests? Is there a chance that at some future time the yarn about the Popess Joan will cease to be myth and become fact?

It is not easy for a man, a man who is a priest, a priest who grumpily finds himself in his middle years, to maintain a proper calm in the presence of these questions. Detachment has its limits.

There is nothing to be gained by talking, in the present context, about the battle of the sexes or the emancipation of women or the misogynism of St. Paul or the closed world—and maybe minds—of the celibate Roman Catholic clergy. We propose that the true question is this: Does a woman become a more perfectly evolved and therefore more personally contented human being, and therefore a more beneficent influence in the world, by the simple process of doing more and more of the things that men do? The executive's chair, the hiring and the firing, the manipulation of money, the smoke-filled room, the double dry martini, the three-hour lunch, the title on the door and the ankle-deep rugs on the floor—is all this the cherished dream, the shining apex of fulfillment, the supreme happiness of womankind, A.D. 1968? Will Desdemona never rest till she has grown a beard, and must Juliet train to be a jockey?

There is an old-fashioned idea that nature itself, through the very physical and psychic composition of the sexes, has given some sort of hint as to a most efficient and generally satisfying division of the labors of this world between the sexes. There are so many functions that women, guided by sure instinct, perform far more deftly and skillfully than men: nursing the sick, for example. There are so many imperative jobs that women do expertly and men either cannot or will not do at all: training small children, teaching civilized manners, keeping a house really clean.

Some will ask whether every woman must be confined to the traditionally feminine tasks; will no woman be permitted to discharge any of the larger functions in this world? To which query a double answer could be made. First, a simple negative. There are not a few individual women who should and will be doctors, lawyers, business tycoons, judges, senators and college presidents. Splendid. We admire them, we wish them well, we will be properly attentive when they speak. The second answer is a question. What *are* the larger tasks in this world?

It is a mere man who writes. But if he were given a choice between raising seven children and heading a university, he would not hesitate for a split second. Universities are very difficult places, to be sure, but somehow manageable.

Bright Eschatology

*And they will see the Son of Man coming upon the clouds
of heaven, with great power and glory; and he will send
out his angels with a loud blast of the trumpet, to gather
his elect from the four winds, from one end of heaven to
the other.* (Matthew 34:30–31; Gospel of the Last Sunday
after Pentecost)

The end of the world: the very concept is electrifying.
How strange it is that the old apocalyptic vision of fiery,
universal cataclysm should live again as the hideous, sober
prospect of a nuclear age. We think of total destruction as
possible and possibly imminent because of the findings of
science. The early Christians thought in identical terms,
though with different feelings, because of the words of
Christ.

The eschatological statements of the Saviour are recorded by all three Synoptics—there is nothing of the
kind in the Gospel whose author also wrote the Apocalypse
—and some at least of the sayings are unquestionably
authentic words of our Lord. It is equally beyond question
that the primitive Christians lived in keen expectation of
what Shakespeare, long after, called "the promised end."
Now, some two thousand years later, the end is not yet.

What, therefore, is the doctrinal content, as distinct from the apocalyptic language, of these eschatological discourses of Him who is Himself truth and way and life?

First, Christ teaches that human history has a term, that mankind has an appointed destiny. The profound significance of this truth (it is the basis of Christian optimism) is immediately evident. If the story of mankind has a conclusion that is a genuine denouement and not merely a running-down or burning-out, then the story of mankind makes sense. Rational existence becomes exactly that, and every human life, instead of being a disconnected series of incidents and accidents amounting to tragic absurdity, is a meaningful progress toward what not only must be, but should be. Wholehearted Christians have little idea of the secret torment of many in this world— the torment of absolute and final and irredmediable insignificance.

Second, Christ declares unequivocally—and not only in the passages now under consideration—that He, who was in this world and would leave this world, will return to this world. He is clear as to the manner of that last epiphany. He will return not as the lowly and despised Galilean, but in kingly majesty, *upon the clouds of heaven, with great power and glory;* not as the Prophet-Messiah, but as supreme Judge. He will then establish in its perfection that *kingdom* of which He so often spoke and whose ultimate triumph He promised.

What more of Christian doctrine is contained in the eschatological discourse? Will the world as we know it be consumed in fire? We do not know. The language of Christ here is, as Msgr. Knox notes, "oracular." He is deliberately employing the awe-inspiring images of Jewish apocalyptic literature. Will the world as we know it be destroyed at all? We do not know. Is the coming of Christ any way imminent, may it be expected in the near future? We do not know.

On this last Sunday of the ecclesiastical year, even as another precious calendar year moves somberly to its conclusion, the friend of Christ will listen cheerfully to his Friend's solemn words. Life will end—but as it should. Christ will come as Judge—but to reward as well as punish.